The Pageant of Music

The Pageant of Music

An Introduction to the History of Music

ALAN BLACKWOOD

Foreword by Percy M. Young
Illustrations by Christine Skilton

BARRIE & JENKINS
COMMUNICA - EUROPA

© Alan Blackwood 1977

First published in 1977 by
Barrie and Jenkins Ltd
24 Highbury Crescent London N5 1RX

ISBN 0 214 20423 5

Printed in Great Britain at the Alden Press, Oxford

Foreword

Every so often in the affairs of mankind some combination of ideas and feelings takes place, to cause such alterations in modes of thinking, and in action, that civilisation is seen to take a new turning. Across the centuries empires have given way before the onrush of new thought; great movements have come and gone; and great men and women too. Today we live in an age of greatest change, and we know that the world of tomorrow will be vastly different from the world of now.

At the present time three factors are especially significant. First, we live in a period of revolutionary technological advance. Second, because of ease of travel and the spread of information, we live in a contracting world; for instance, to anyone now living in London, New York or Moscow are nearer than Glasgow and Edinburgh were to a Londoner of 150 years ago. Third, in Britain as in the United States, we live in a multiracial and multicultural society. Within each of these basic features of modern life, music is somewhere to be found. On the one hand it acts as a stimulus, on the other as a reflection.

This is why there are new kinds of music, collectively labelled 'modern music'. But as we look back through history we discover that for those living at any time there was 'modern music'; music, that is, that was different in form and quality from previous kinds of music. It should, however, be said that in the contest between new and old—this applies to all the arts—the new more often than not stole some of the clothes of the old.

When we look further we know that each individual possesses his own kind of music. For music begins with the individual. It begins with the exercise of the voice—and it comes into being before language. Indeed, language—as Plato proposed long ago—is a form of music. Music begins also with the movements of the body. When, comparatively late in time, the first attempts to show musical sounds graphically were made, the notation employed pictured the rise and fall of the voice. When it was desired to measure time in music, the yardstick was the beat of the human heart.

By some quite marvellous means, human sounds, augmented by other sounds of nature, take shape into music and convey meaning. Sometimes meaning is strengthened by words, sometimes by action. Song, dance, ritual music, work music, entertainment music come into existence. All of this goes across centuries. With the passage of time creative musical artists emerged, and more and more individual composers and performers stamped their authority—derived in part from a common stock of musical experience—on places and periods.

This whole process is what makes the story of music, which comes before us like a passing show—as the title of this book suggests. The title is well chosen, for a pageant is a parade of people. Music is people, in that it contains the ideas, feelings and musical idioms of different peoples of diverse times, traditions and places. It is a wonderful expression of the essence of living.

Alan Blackwood takes the themes I have put forward and dresses them with the realities of the music we perform and hear. He deals with a multitude of ideas that are profound, and often difficult to understand; but by clear and patient explanation he helps us to meet the challenge with confidence. What is equally important, he conveys a sense of pleasure in music. In former days it was thought not quite proper to do this; but I comfort myself with the thought that without pleasure in living (and music is one of the chief pleasures) there is little point in living. I find that Alan Blackwood—whose own tastes are wide-ranging—emphasises the pleasure in togetherness that music develops. In so doing he tells us—as it is said today—'what music is all about'.

P.M.Y.

Music has been a thing of magic and wonder to people of all times and places. Indian and Chinese legends tell of musicians who could create fire or water, or even change the seasons, by means of their potent and mysterious art. The Old Testament of the Bible tells the story of how the sound of horns and trumpets was supposed to have brought down the mighty walls of Jericho. Orpheus, one of the most famous figures in Greek mythology, could tame the wildest beasts with the sound of his voice, or the notes of his lyre.

The wonderful properties ascribed to music is why people everywhere have associated it with heaven. The people of pre-Christian Mexico, for example, believed that their gods had built a special bridge to convey music from heaven to earth. And all over the world, people of different races and civilisations have given music a special place in their acts of worship, believing that music, and often dancing as well, would bring them into the closest contact with their gods.

The Greeks of antiquity, who were very poetic people, considered music to be a divine gift, transmitted through the wind, the roar or murmur of the ocean waves, and other sounds of nature. They made a special kind of harp—the aeolian harp—which was designed to be placed in the open air, where it could receive this divine music born along by the wind, and re-create it through its singing strings. In other cases, it was the muses, daughters of the supreme god Zeus, who were believed to help men interpret the divine sounds of nature through their songs and dances. The word 'music' comes from this.

Pythagoras, the celebrated Greek thinker from the province of Sicily, shared a widespread belief of his time that the source of music lay in the stars and planets. He coupled this with an equally widespread belief in the magical properties of numbers, and was sure that a relationship must exist between the 'Music of the Spheres' and the meaning of numbers. Few people today take seriously the idea of a 'Music of the Spheres' or the occult science of numerology. But Pythagoras's investigation into the relationship between musical sounds and mathematical numbers was based on secure scientific fact.

Sounds are pulses, or vibrations, set up in the air (or water) by a vibrating object. When they reach our ears they make our ear drums vibrate at the same rate, and our brains interpret the

Pythagoras demonstrating the relationship between pitch and numbers, taken from a renaissance treatise on musical theory

vibrations as sound. These sound waves, as they are usually called, can vibrate at many different speeds, and such speeds, or *frequencies,* can be accurately measured. For example, the note A by which musicians tune their instruments before a concert has a frequency of 440. That particular note produces 440 vibrations, or sound waves, per second. If a sound wave has a faster, or higher frequency than this, then its *pitch* will sound correspondingly higher to the ear. If the frequency is lower, then so will be the pitch of the sound by a precisely related degree. Anyone can discover this scientific principle by stretching a piece of string or an elastic band. They can see, as well as hear, that as they stretch the string more tightly so it vibrates more rapidly and produces a higher-pitched sound.

In addition to this basic mathematical relationship between frequency and pitch there is the question of the quality, or *tone* of a sound, which can be similarly analysed. All sounds, in fact, are mixtures of sounds of different pitch and intensity. From any such mixture one sound makes the greatest impact on the listener's ear and mind. This is called the *fundamental,* and gives the note its particular pitch. All the other sounds above or below the fundamental affect the special quality of that note. These are the *overtones,* and it is they which make an instrument such as the violin sound quite different from a trombone, even when they are playing notes of exactly the same pitch, or our voices all sound different from each other.

People have used sounds in various ways to produce music. In Eastern countries, musicians use intervals which are much smaller than those generally used in Western, or European music. An *interval* in music means the degree of difference in pitch between two notes. And people in countries like India generally sing much more through their noses than people in Western countries, who are taught to open their mouths wide when they sing.

Despite such differences in method and style, musical instruments from all over the world have much in common. They are all designed to produce vibrations and to amplify and modify these vibrations by means of *resonance.* Resonance occurs when one object, or part of the same object, vibrates 'in sympathy' with another. A window pane, for example, might accidentally vibrate in sympathy with the sound of a passing car. In a musical instrument, the size and shape of the instrument itself, and the materials it is made from, all enter into the process of resonance.

Musical scholars—musicologists—have classified instruments under four headings, using suitably descriptive Greek words.

Idiophones are instruments made from wood or metal, both excellent materials for generating sound when they are struck. The simplest of all instruments, a wooden block, is an idiophone. So is the xylophone, and all kinds of cymbal, gong or bell.

Membranophones are instruments made by stretching a membrane, traditionally a portion of dried animal skin, across a resonating structure. All kinds of drum belong to this class of instrument.

Aerophones are all instruments fashioned into the shape of a tube or funnel, in which the player sets up a vibrating column of air with his own breath. Instruments ranging from the flimsiest reed flute to the most beautifully fashioned trumpet or horn are aerophones.

Chordophones have a stretched string, or strings, as the basis of their sound, and include all instruments of the violin type, where the strings are made to vibrate by being scraped with a bow, and other instruments, like the harp or guitar, where they are plucked.

An alternative system of classification, the one usually referred to in any discussion to do with the instruments of an orchestra, uses four other headings.

Percussion instruments, designed to be struck, include virtually all the instruments otherwise classed as idiophones and membranophones.

Stringed instruments correspond almost exactly to chordophones, as a particular group of instruments.

Woodwind instruments are aerophones which require the player to breathe across the section of a tube, or breathe across a thin reed, in order to create a vibrating column of air. Modern woodwind instruments (not necessarily made of wood) include the flute, oboe, clarinet, saxophone and bassoon.

Brass instruments are other aerophones requiring the action of the player's own lips at one end of the tube to create the vibrating column of air. Brass instruments include the trumpet, trombone, horn and tuba.

There are many representations in stone, or in the paintings found in such places as the tombs of the Egyptian pharaohs, to show that the basic design of musical instruments has not radically changed in four or five thousand years. A few examples of the instruments themselves have survived, including a trumpet found in the tomb of the pharaoh Tutankhamen. The sound it makes has been recorded and it seems quite similar to a modern trumpet. The tantalising thing for scholars is that while there is plenty of evidence about the musical instruments of ancient times, their appearance and capabilities, there is no way of knowing exactly what kind of melodies, harmonies and rhythms the musicians of the time extracted from them. For sounds fade back into the air as

Egyptian musicians and dancers, based on wall paintings of about 1400–1300 B.C.

quickly as they are created, and there is no surviving musical tradition going that far back in time to keep alive the character or spirit of the music. Scholars have found what they think is a form of Egyptian musical writing, but they cannot tell what notes or tunes it signifies.

Even in the case of the Greeks, who left behind them so much other evidence of their civilisation, relatively little is known about the kind of music they actually played and sang. What has survived is a knowledge of their musical theories and techniques.

The Greeks based their music on a number of *scales*. The word 'scale' comes from the Italian *scala,* meaning a 'step' or 'stairway', and describes any sequence of notes which goes up or down in pitch by a particular series of intervals, or steps. Scales are the building blocks of music—the notes made available to those wishing to create a piece of music.

One kind of scale, common to much folk music—traditional songs and dances of ordinary people—is called the *pentatonic* scale, meaning, in Greek, a sequence of five tones, or notes. These notes happen to correspond, as far as pitch intervals are concerned, to any five consecutive notes played on the black keys of a piano. The Greeks themselves favoured sequences of four notes which made up what they called a *tetrachord*. Their scales, or *modes,* were built up from these tetrachords, and they are significant in musical history because some of their features were carried over into the music of the Christian era.

The development of European culture was for hundreds of years very strongly influenced by the Christian church. The first Christian communities were in the region of Palestine, where Christ himself lived, and in parts of North Africa. But in the fourth century A.D., the Roman Emperor Constantine was converted to Christianity, and he encouraged its growth within the Roman Empire. Rome itself became one of the most important centres of church administration, and missionaries like St Augustine carried the new religion to other parts of Europe.

The music used by this branch of the church, later to become known as the Roman Catholic Church, was a kind of chanting. The principle of chanting is common to many religions. It played a big part in the worship of the Jews, as described in the Old Testament, and some of the earliest Christian chanting was taken directly from Judaism. St Ambrose, Bishop of Milan, who lived during the fourth century, was one of the first church administrators, and under his supervision a distinctive form of chant was introduced for use in churches throughout Christendom. Either during, or a little after Ambrose's own lifetime, this type of chant became based on the notes of four scales which, in their turn, were based on the structure of the old Greek modes. Two hundred years later, an even more famous church leader and administrator, Pope Gregory I, approved the addition of four more scales, or modes, for use in musical acts of worship. The four original modes were then called the *authentic* modes, and the four newer ones, closely related to them, were called the *plagal* modes. Hundreds of years later still, in the 16th century, a Swiss monk, Henry of Glarus, or Henricus Glareanus, wrote a book about the church modes and gave them the old Greek names, such as the Dorian, Lydian and Aeolian modes, although they did not correspond to the Greek originals.

The special kind of chanting based upon the church modes was called *plainchant*, or *plainsong*, and was used to set to music the words of the liturgy—the words of the church services. The line of the melody, moving gently up and down the notes of one of the modes, was sung in *unison* (everybody singing the same note). It followed the stress and flow of the words and so had no regular beat. Those who used the Ambrosian and Gregorian chants did not compose music in the modern sense of the word. They established a formal pattern of singing. Nor was this kind of music intended to be listened to for its own sake. It was part of the fabric of church life, like the walls and windows of the church itself or the vestments of the priest. But it remained the principal kind of European music for hundreds of years, regularly sung in churches and monasteries during the period sometimes known as the 'Dark Ages'. This was the period which followed the break-up of the Roman Empire, when Western Europe was often invaded and plundered by barbarian tribes from further east, when plague and famine devastated whole populations, and the churches and monasteries were the only surviving centres of art and learning.

However, the inventiveness of men did bring about some changes in plainsong. They started to elaborate upon it, by adding sequences of notes in support of a particular word or phrase in the liturgy, or by inserting words into the liturgy to help sustain a part of the melody. Such elaborations were called *tropes*. Much more significant was the introduction of a kind of part-singing called *organum*. This was a real departure from the original plainsong, involving the simultaneous singing of two lines of melody. At its simplest, organum was the singing of two notes always at the same interval of pitch apart. This could be compared to the two parallel lines of a railway track, faithfully following each other round every curve. More advanced forms of organum involved changes in the pitch intervals, so that two distinct lines of melody were sounded together.

Organum was historically of great importance, because it led into one of the most enduring styles or systems of Western music—*polyphony*. This is a Greek word meaning 'many sounds', in contrast to the *monophony*, or 'single sound' of plainsong. It involves the weaving together of two or more lines of melody, and demonstrates one great difference between the nature of words and of music. For if one person starts reciting a passage of words, and then other people join in, there is soon confusion, whatever plan might be followed. But if that person should start singing, and his friends join in according to an agreed plan, the music becomes more meaningful, not less. Instead of confusion there is order and a new understanding. An early type of polyphonic composition was the conductus, a title which comes from the Latin word *conducere* ('to bring together' or 'unite'). The conductus, like other early kinds of polyphonic music, had a leading melodic line, known as the *cantus firmus*, or 'fixed song', to which other melodic parts were added. Our word 'tenor' comes from this type of music, because *tenere* means 'to hold' or 'maintain', and the *cantus firmus* was usually given to the singer with the highest voice, who held it above the other melodic parts. Another important thing was that in a conductus this melody was often specially composed, instead of simply being extracted from plainsong.

Such music could not be taken for granted, as something that merely acted in support of the liturgy or any other text. It took on a life of its own, and drew attention to the musicians who created it. No longer were they anonymous monks or choristers but men who began to be spoken of by name. Two of the earliest to be accorded such recognition were Leonin (about 1130–1180) and Perotin (about 1200–1250), or Leoninus and Perotinus, to give the Latin form of their names. Both were church choirmasters in Paris closely associated with the cathedral of Notre Dame, one of the great cathedrals then being built in the Gothic style in France, England and other parts of Europe. Leonin wrote a *Great Book of Organum* containing music for use throughout the church year.

Polyphony introduced three important new technical features to church music. Firstly, the simultaneous sounding of two notes of different pitch in organum had already produced what is called *harmony*. The combination of two or more melodic lines, or parts, in polyphonic music made for correspondingly more varied and interesting harmonies. Secondly, the process of making the melodic lines fit happily together started another great musical method called *counterpoint* (from the Latin *punctus contra punctum* meaning 'note against note'). Thirdly, the need to support such counterpoint with a steady pulse, or beat, brought about a fresh attitude to *rhythm*, which had not been of any consequence in plainsong.

For the performance of plainsong, musicians had sometimes written signs or accents called *neumes* above the words to be sung. These were only a general guide as to how the melodic line should proceed, and did not even indicate the actual pitch of the notes to be sung. Polyphonic music required something more scientific than this. So musicians developed a new and more precise system of writing the music down, to help the composer think out his ideas, and enable others to learn the music accurately and rehearse it together.

Any system of writing music down, whereby musical sounds of different pitch are represented as notes, is called *notation*. The system devised by musicians in the early days of polyphony is called *staff notation*. It was based on the idea of a horizontal line, or lines, indicating precise degrees of pitch. By placing dots or squares to represent individual notes, on or between these lines, called staff lines, or staves, an accurate record of the notes of a piece of music could be set down. By changing the shape of these dots or squares, their relative duration could also be shown.

An 11th-century Italian monk named Guido, from the town of Arezzo, was a pioneer figure in the field of notation. He also thought of a special way of naming notes, based on the syllables of a well-known plainsong hymn to John the Baptist. The purpose of this was to help singers memorise the music—an ingenious idea which has been used again in the modern *tonic sol fa* system, by which the familiar sounds 'doh ray me fah soh lah tee doh' indicate the relationship between the notes in any scale and any piece of music using that scale. Musical notation, and other valuable aids to musical theory and practice, owe a great deal to Guido and his friends.

So much European music in the Middle Ages, like so much painting, sculpture and architecture, was religious because the Church was the most powerful institution. The way in which the towers, spires and flying buttresses of the great Gothic cathedrals rose high above the roof tops of any medieval town or city was a telling symbol of that power. But even people who lived in their shadow, and really did believe in the flames of everlasting hell fire, still liked to sing and dance and enjoy life when they could. The Church itself recognised this, and the many religious feasts and festivals were a welcome opportunity for merry-making. There were even such events as the so-called Feast of Fools, during which church clerics made fun of religious ceremonies in a way that would be considered quite sacrilegious today.

Much of the entertainment on such occasions, though, was provided by travelling musicians who were not attached to any church institution. They were often very energetic and versatile people who could juggle and perform acrobatics as well as sing, dance and play a variety of musical instruments. Sometimes they also had performing animals like dogs and bears. In France they were known as *jongleurs*, a word describing a kind of juggler, and in parts of Germany they bore the equivalent German name of *Gaukler*. These *Gaukler* had a recognised costume of yellow and red with sometimes a kind of cap with little bells attached to it. Some adopted special names, such as *Regenbogen* ('Rainbow'), and one chronicler of the time said that they could 'play the drum, the cymbals and the hurdy-gurdy; throw small apples and catch knives; perform card tricks and jump through four hoops'.

The troubadours of southern France were also entertainers, but they performed at the courts of the nobility rather than in the market place. Indeed, many of them were kings or princes themselves, and they sang songs of love and knightly chivalry. This was the time of the Crusades, and if they had been crusaders themselves—as was the case with Richard *Coeur de Lion* ('The Lionheart'), also King Richard I of England—they gave accounts of their adventures and acts of valour in *chansons de geste* ('songs of deeds').

The word 'troubadour' comes from the old Provençal word *trobar* meaning 'to find', in the sense of discovering or making up verses and tunes. In other parts of France similar poet-musicians

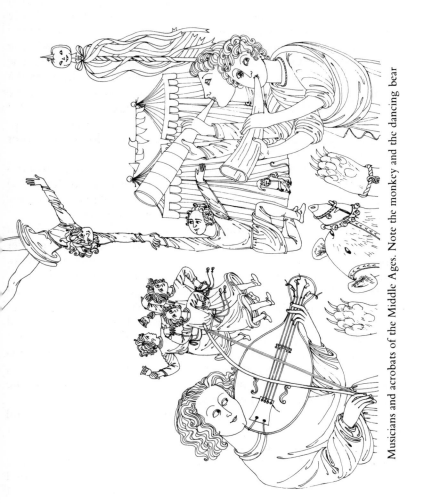

Musicians and acrobats of the Middle Ages. Note the monkey and the dancing bear

were called by the equivalent French word of *trouvères*. In Germany they were known as *minnesinger* ('singers of love'). Walter von der Vogelweide (about 1170–1230) is the best remembered of these *minnesinger*. They had a reputation for being more scholarly and serious in their treatment of words and music than the troubadours and *trouvères*, and met together to hold song contests of the kind described in Wagner's opera *Tannhäuser*. The bards and minstrels of Celtic Britain also held competitions in the arts of poetry and music. The most notable of these events were the *Eistedfodds* of Wales, which continue to this day.

All this music comes under the heading of *secular* (non-religious) music, and secular and religious music gradually came closer together during the Middle Ages.

A famous piece of medieval polyphonic music demonstrates very clearly this blending of the religious and the secular. It is called the Reading Rota, and was composed at Reading Abbey some time during the 13th century, probably by a monk named John of Fornsete. A rota is a musical round, or canon, in which different voices or instruments join in with the same tune one after the other in a way that allows the tune to follow itself round and round. From a purely technical point of view the Reading Rota was a very advanced piece of music for its time. Just as significant is the fact that it was supplied with two alternative texts. One was a religious text in Latin for use of the piece in church. The other was in Old English, starting with the words 'Sumer is icumen in' ('Summer's coming'), for secular performance. Many other medieval compositions were similarly designed to accommodate two texts, a religious one in Latin, and a secular text in the vernacular (the everyday language of the people).

The music itself, at this time, began to combine religious and secular styles. Melodies for church use were often a mixture of plainsong and the kinds of tune sung by the troubadours, *trouvères* and other minstrels. This situation continued for a long time. The tune of one old Provençal song called *L'homme armé* ('The Armed Man') became a particular favourite with renaissance composers for use in their masses, motets and other church compositions.

Such a broadening of the scope and character of music came under the heading of *ars nova* ('new art'), in contrast to the *ars antiqua* ('old art') of earlier composers like Leonin and Perotin.

Bagpipe player. Bagpipes are an ancient type of instrument, played in many parts of Europe and the Middle East

Two composers of the *ars nova* period were Philippe de Vitry (about 1291–1361), who is thought to have invented the term, and Guillaume de Machaut (about 1300–1377). The latter was especially concerned that, as well as being technically interesting, his music should sound sweet and pleasing to the ear. 'I have listened to it several times,' he wrote of one of his compositions, 'and it pleases me very well.'

During the next century there followed a whole group of composers who extended these principles, practices and ideas. They are known as the Burgundians because they were either born in, or spent much of their lives in, the kingdom of Burgundy. At its greatest extent in the 14th and 15th centuries Burgundy covered most of what is today eastern and north-eastern France, Belgium and Holland (The Netherlands). One of the leading figures of this Burgundian group, or school, of musicians was the English-born John Dunstable (about 1385–1453). Others who came a little after him were Gilles Binchois (1400–1460), Guillaume Dufay (1400–1474), Johannes (Jean de) Ockeghem (1425–1495) and his pupil Josquin des Près (1450–1521).

Guillaume Dufay and Gilles Binchois as depicted on an illuminated manuscript

Western Europe at this time was recovering from the devastating effects of the bubonic plague, the Black Death. And there was a series of bitter and destructive wars between England and France, known collectively as the Hundred Years War, during which Henry V won the Battle of Agincourt and Joan of Arc raised the Siege of Orleans. There was, however, a much brighter side to life. Interest in the arts and sciences was quickening, scholars, artists and musicians travelled widely and were welcomed everywhere. Burgundy itself was a thriving kingdom, noted for the colour and pageantry of its court, and the Burgundian musicians were some of the most successful and prominent men of their age. Dunstable was a celebrated mathematician and astrologer as well as a musician. Binchois was both a high ranking member of the clergy and an official at the court of Burgundy. Dufay and Josquin des Près served in the Papal Chapel in Rome. Ockeghem, in service to the French court, was acclaimed 'The Prince of Music' in his own day and attracted a wide circle of scholars with his new theories and methods, much as Schoenberg was to do five hundred years later. The way in which they travelled, exchanged ideas and took an active interest in many subjects and occupations typified them as men of the Renaissance.

Renaissance is a French word meaning 're-birth', and refers to a re-awakening among European scholars of interest in aspects of art, philosophy and literature which had been largely forgotten about since the civilisations of Greece and Rome. It inspired a tremendous upsurge of artistic, literary and scientific activity which began in Italy and spread across Western Europe during the 15th and 16th centuries. It also encouraged people to look with fresh minds at themselves and the world about them.

For hundreds of years the Church had dominated European life and thought. It had focused attention upon itself and its fundamental teaching about the life to come. During the Renaissance the Church lost a good deal of this power and influence. The whole spirit of the age made intelligent and creative men, like the astronomer Galileo Galilei, restless in their quest for knowledge, and this led them to challenge church leaders on matters of doctrine. Other renaissance men and women, like the Medici family in Florence, took away from the Church its traditional and previously almost exclusive role as patron of learning and the arts, by employing artists on their own account.

There was also serious disruption within the Church itself. A German monk, Martin Luther (1483–1546), rebelled against what he saw as abuses in the conduct of church life. He and those who joined with him wished to reform the life and practices of the Church. Their movement was called the Reformation. Their actions led to the creation, at the cost of much bitterness, bloodshed and war between whole nations, of the Protestant churches—those churches which protested against the authority of the Church of Rome.

Despite all these reverses and disruptions, religion still played a very important part in European life, and some of the finest church music was composed during the renaissance period. One of Luther's own aims in the Reformation was to allow church congregations to share more fully in acts of worship through the use of music. 'Music drives away the Devil and makes people happy,' he wrote, and composed hymn tunes, or chorales, to words in the vernacular, for them to sing. *Ein' feste Burg* ('A Sure Defence', also called 'A Mighty Fortress Is Our God') is the best known of these chorales, still sung regularly in Lutheran church services.

Such ideas prompted the Catholic Church to reform many of its own practices and attitudes in a movement called the Counter-Reformation. As an important part of this movement, the Church convened a reforming body called the Council of Trent, and one of the things this council did was to criticize much polyphonic music for being too elaborate. Such music, it decreed, should not 'give empty pleasure to the ear' but should be written 'so that the words may be clearly understood by all'.

A composer who accepted these criticisms and acted upon them was Giovanni Pierluigi da Palestrina (about 1525–1594). He was on the Papal staff for much of his life, and there is a story that it was only the heaven-inspired beauty of his *Missa Papae Marcellus* ('Mass for Pope Marcellus') which prevented the Church from banning music altogether from its services. There is no historical evidence to support this story, but Palestrina certainly did write music which sounded particularly clear and pure and so helped to restore music to favour within the Catholic Church. Many composers of later generations have praised the qualities of Palestrina's music. Three hundred years later Wagner wrote of it as 'timeless and spaceless, a spiritual revelation throughout'. Another dedicated composer of the Counter-Reformation was Spanish-born Tomas Luis de Victoria (about 1548–1611), whose name is sometimes given in the Italianised version Vittoria. For many listeners his music expresses the intense devotion which the Spanish people have always felt towards their religion.

Both Palestrina and Victoria composed settings of the Mass, the principal service of the Catholic Church, and numerous motets. These motets were not settings of the official words of the church service—the liturgy. They were special kinds of sacred song, or *cantiones sacrae* as they were called in Latin, intended to be performed during those parts of the Mass when there was a pause in the recital of the actual liturgy, as when the priest was consecrating the sacraments. The Mass itself has inspired composers over a longer period of European musical history than practically any other form or idea. The form most frequently set to music is that known as the 'Ordinary' of the Mass and which consists of five parts called, in Latin, *Kyrie, Gloria, Credo, Sanctus* with *Benedictus*, and *Agnus Dei*. The Requiem Mass in memory of the dead (*requiem* means 'repose') is a special form of the service which composers have also set to music down the centuries.

In England the conflict between Catholics and Protestants was as fierce as in any other part of Europe. John Taverner (about 1495–1545) was one composer whose life was unhappily affected by these troubles. As a young man Taverner was appointed by Cardinal Wolsey to the post of choirmaster and organist at what is now Christ Church Cathedral, Oxford, where he wrote the Catholic church music for which he is famous. Then he became a Protestant, and after a period of imprisonment took a part in the dissolution of the monasteries as decreed by Henry VIII. He regretted the beautiful music he had earlier written, describing it bitterly as 'Popish ditties written in the time of my blindness.' Other composers who lived through this Tudor period of English history were not quite so badly upset by events. Thomas Tallis (about 1505–1585) saw the Catholic liturgy in Latin replaced by services in English, then return to Latin, and finally go back to English again, as different religious factions struggled for ascendancy. Such things certainly disturbed Tallis, but he was still able to write some of the finest church music of the English renaissance period, including one of the most remarkable of all polyphonic compositions, a Latin motet to the words *Spem in alium* with forty separate parts divided between eight small choirs of five voices each. William Byrd (1543–1623), pupil and friend of Tallis, was a Catholic who also managed to adapt himself to the changing times. For the Catholic service Byrd composed many beautiful Latin motets, and for the newly established Church of England he wrote similar pieces set to English words, called anthems.

The really significant thing about the renaissance period, however, was the growth of secular art, literature and music. In the case of both literature and music this was greatly helped by the invention of printing, which made possible the distribution of books or notated sheet music on a scale quite unknown in the Middle Ages when all such material had to be painstakingly copied out by hand. In the case of music, other technical advances led to many improvements in the design and construction of musical instruments, while increasing prosperity through the growth in trade and commerce gave more and more people the opportunity to perform music in their own homes. This was the first great age of secular 'art' music—music consciously thought out and composed—and many new musical forms and styles grew out of it.

One such form was the madrigal, a type of song for a small group of singers. The madrigal originated in Italy, where it was called the *madriale* or *mandriale*, and grew out of earlier kinds of secular song. One of these earlier types of song was known as the *caccia*, the Italian word for 'hunt' or 'chase', because the individual vocal parts chased each other round and round in the style of a canon. Another earlier type of song was the frotolla. This was almost like a simple madrigal, and represented a significant step forward by making sure that the main line of the melody was always sung by the highest voice so that the tune itself could be clearly heard throughout. Francesco Landini (about 1325–1397), who was blind from childhood, was a celebrated composer of these forerunners of the madrigal and of early examples of the madrigal itself.

Two of the first great madrigalists were Flemish-born composers who spent much of their lives in Italy—Adriaan Willaert (about 1480–1562) and Orlando di Lasso, or Lassus (1530–1594). Both also wrote some of the finest renaissance religious music. Italian madrigalists of the period included Luca Marenzio (1553–1599), Giovanni Dalla Croce (about 1557–1609), Carlo Gesualdo (about 1560–1615) and Monteverdi (discussed later). Even composers like Palestrina, who dedicated their lives and work to the church, also wrote some madrigals. The outstanding feature of this music is how strongly it conveys the emotions expressed by the words. People revealed their feelings much more openly in renaissance times than today, and life could be a passionate and sometimes a dangerous affair, as the action of such a play as *Romeo and Juliet*, set in renaissance Italy, makes very clear. Gesualdo, for example, killed his wife and her lover. Feelings of sorrow and despair, joy and happiness, are all conveyed in these madrigals with a strength and directness that was quite new to the art of music then, and has rarely been equalled since. The whole idea of happy or sad music, as we think of it today, really dates from this time.

The popularity of madrigal singing quickly spread from Italy to other parts of Europe, notably to England. This prompted

Nicholas Yonge, a singer at St Paul's cathedral in London, to issue a collection of Italian madrigals in translation which he entitled *Musica Transalpina* ('Music from across the Alps'). Byrd, Thomas Morley (1557–1603), John Wilbye (1577–1638), Thomas Weelkes (about 1580–1623), Orlando Gibbons (1583–1625) and others then composed large numbers of madrigals of their own. One famous collection was published under the title *The Triumphs of Oriana*, the name 'Oriana' fancifully referring to Queen Elizabeth I. These men were contemporaries of Shakespeare, and the way in which their madrigals expressed both human feelings and a special feeling for the English countryside, made this a great age for English music as well as literature.

Madrigals were still largely polyphonic, or contrapuntal, in the way they were written. Each singer weaved his or her line of melody in with the rest. But musicians realised that a person singing on their own could exploit qualities of the human voice, in terms of agility and the expression of emotion, which were not possible when a whole choir or even quite a small ensemble were singing inter-related parts. So another kind of secular song developed, in England called an 'ayre', in which only one vocalist rendered the melody. The other singers provided a quite separate accompaniment, or the accompaniment was provided by an instrument. The most eminent Elizabethan composer of these songs, or ayres, was John Dowland (1563–1626). He wrote most of his songs with a lute accompaniment. Dowland was a most successful man, who served the royal courts of Denmark and England, and had his music published in eight different cities, which was a tremendous achievement in his day. The tone of his songs, though, is generally sad and wistful. Dowland also wrote much music for the lute on its own, and he and other lutenists frequently made special arrangements for their instrument of existing songs and dances.

The lute, a beautiful looking stringed instrument, plucked like a guitar, was just one of the many instruments to be found in the homes of the wealthy during the 15th and 16th centuries. People were particularly fond of making music with whole sets of the same basic instrument, each member of the set or 'family' being made to a different size, to encompass a differently pitched range of notes, corresponding quite closely to the voices—bass, tenor, alto,

Renaissance lute and viol players

soprano—in a choir. A very popular stringed instrument of this type, played with a bow, was the viol. Another was the woodwind recorder. Musicians playing a whole group of such instruments formed what was known as a 'consort' (an old spelling of the word 'concert'), and the instruments themselves were often proudly displayed, in a special case, in the owner's home.

One of the earliest types of keyboard instrument was also developed during the renaissance period. This was the virginal, an instrument small enough to be carried from room to room and placed on any convenient table or shelf. The virginal and early versions of other keyboard instruments like the harpsichord were often elaborately decorated, a favourite feature being a graceful scene from Greek mythology painted on the lid. An early composer of keyboard music was Antonio de Cabezón (1510–1566), who served the Spanish court and was reputedly blind from birth. In England a famous collection of renaissance keyboard pieces, originally written and compiled for a particular family to learn and enjoy, was the *FitzWilliam Virginal Book*.

Brass instruments, no less than stringed, woodwind and keyboard instruments, benefited from the greater skills and ingenuity of renaissance craftsmen. Trumpets, used for signalling in battle, were played, often with a fine array of drums, for grand ceremonial occasions in times of peace. For many centuries, going right back to Biblical days, trumpets had had one very long, straight tube. Renaissance craftsmen started to make trumpets with a tube carefully bent double, thus making it a much more convenient instrument to handle. The trombone was an even more interesting brass instrument of the time. The technical significance of these early trombones, or sackbuts as they were called in England, was that they had a sliding valve by which the player could alter the effective playing length of the tube. A brass instrument with a non–adjustable tube has a rather limited range of notes, starting with its principal note and going up in pitch by a series of notes called its harmonic series. The pitch intervals between the notes in such a series are wide at the lower end, and get closer together as the player reaches the higher notes. With a trombone's adjustable tube, the player could achieve a much fuller range of notes.

The notable developments that took place in music during the renaissance period—a clearer division between melody and harmony, and the growing importance of instrumental music—plus the great revival of interest in the art and literature of Greece and Rome, all contributed to the new art form of opera.

Opera is a combination of music and drama. Other ways of combining these two performing arts had existed before. In the Middle Ages there were religious pageants called Miracle Plays, often performed on the steps of cathedrals and churches. These involved acting and singing of a sort. Much further back in history there was the drama of Greece itself, which included a group of singers, known as the 'chorus', who commented upon the action of the play. Sometimes there was dancing as well. In fact, it was the example of classical Greek drama which brought about the beginnings of opera as we know it today.

These beginnings are found in the activities of a group of Italian noblemen, poets and musicians who called themselves the *Camerata* ('Fellowship') and who lived in Florence during the 16th and early 17th centuries. They discussed many theories and conducted many experiments in the fields of music, poetry and drama. One particular subject that interested them was classical Greek drama, and how this had originally been performed. They believed that all parts in such performances had been sung, and accordingly adopted this practice in their own revivals of Greek drama. Each part of their productions was sung to a kind of melody called *recitative*, and this was accompanied by instruments playing harmonies made up of chords. Such productions they called *dramma per musica* ('drama through music').

One enterprising member of the *Camerata* was Vincenzo Galileo, father of the astronomer. Another was Jacopo Peri (1561–1633), a priest in the household of the Medici family. His *dramma per musica*, or opera, *Euridice*—based on the famous story from Greek mythology about Orpheus and Eurydice—is generally thought to be the first opera actually to be staged. However, the man who really established opera as an exciting and important new art form was Claudio Monteverdi (1567–1643).

While Monteverdi was a musician at the court of the Duke of Mantua, he set to music another and now more famous version of the Orpheus and Eurydice story, called *Orfeo*. Then he left Mantua to take up the post of Director of Music at St Mark's Basilica in Venice. This building was strongly influenced by the architectural styles of Byzantium, the old capital of the Eastern Orthodox Church, renamed Constantinople and then captured by the Turks in 1453. With its high domes and galleries St Mark's was especially noted for its sound properties, or acoustics. Being in the rich and influential city state of Venice it attracted some of the most eminent renaissance composers, and it inspired them to write music which would exploit these remarkable acoustics. Adriaan Willaert, an earlier choirmaster at St Mark's, his pupil Andrea Gabrieli (about 1510–1586), and Andrea's nephew Giovanni Gabrieli (1557–1612) had all written a special kind of antiphonal music for performance in the Basilica. *Antiphon* is another Greek word meaning 'sounding across'. In this context it describes the method of writing for two or more separate groups of singers or instrumentalists in order to create dramatic contrasts of sound between them.

Monteverdi continued this tradition with some dramatic and exciting antiphonal church music of his own. At the same time, the opening of the world's first public opera houses in Venice encouraged him to develop further his acute sense of drama in the direction of opera. Several of the other operas he wrote are now lost, but two of them have survived: *Il Ritorno d'Ulisse* ('The Return of Ulysses'), being based on another famous story from Greek mythology, and *L'Incoronazione di Poppea* ('The Coronation of Poppaea'), being based on an episode from Roman history concerning the Emperor Nero.

In these operas, and in the earlier *Orfeo*, Monteverdi achieved what the members of the *Camerata* had striven towards—a real increase in the dramatic sense of the words through the use of recitative. In addition, Monteverdi made very imaginative use of instruments, to accompany the singers and generally set the scene. He himself wrote no purely instrumental music. But the origins of the orchestra, as a sizeable group of instrumentalists, and of orchestral music can be traced back to the example of his operas.

The popularity of opera spread very quickly throughout Italy, and then to other parts of Europe. The operas of Antonio Cesti (1623–1669) were performed first in Venice and later in Vienna and Innsbruck, where Cesti served for some years at the Austrian court. More significant was the development of opera in France. This was due largely to the work of Jean-Baptiste Lully (1632–1687). He was born in Italy—Giovanni Battista Lulli—but was taken to France as a child and adopted the French version of his name when it was clear to him where his future lay. This future was at the court of Louis XIV.

Louis XIV ruled France from 1643 to 1715, at a time when it was the most powerful, politically united country in Europe. Because of this, and because of all the other eminent men and women of the age whom he attracted to his court, he was known as *Le Roi Soleil* ('The Sun King'). His most enduring monument is the palace he had built at Versailles, just outside Paris. It is a vast building, surrounded by ornamental gardens, lakes and fountains on a correspondingly grand scale. Such grandeur and spaciousness typifies the spirit of the artistic style called baroque.

Lully was one of the most versatile and successful figures at the court of Versailles, collaborating with other outstanding men of the age, including the dramatist Molière. Some might also call him ruthless, since he used the king's support to obtain a virtual monopoly over the production of operas in Paris and at the court. Fortunately, he used his power to good effect, making a special study of the music of Pietro Francesco Cavalli (1602–1676), one of whose Italian operas had been staged in Paris, then brilliantly adapting his own style to suit French tastes in music and drama. A particular type of French drama was that created by Racine and Corneille, which attached great importance to the pure delivery of the words. Another prevailing taste among the French aristocracy was for elaborately staged ballet sequences, combined with spectacular stage sets. Lully's respect for the special features of the French language, and his frequent use of ballet, established a style of opera in France quite distinct from that to be found in Italy.

Lully also established one basic type of operatic overture. The word 'overture' comes from the French *ouverture*, meaning an 'opening' in the sense of a beginning. The earliest kinds of overture were simply intended as a signal to the audience that the

Baroque opera was often lavishly staged. This is a scene from an early production of Cesti's opera *Il pomo d'oro*

performance was about to begin, and were not very important. Lully wrote overtures which had a slow and stately beginning, then a faster section to create an increasing air of expectancy and excitement, and a concluding slow section to lead into the grand and formal opening of the actual opera.

The musical styles of the court of Versailles were introduced to England by Charles II when he returned from the exile forced on him by the Civil War and the subsequent rule of Oliver Cromwell. English composers of this time included Matthew Locke (about 1630–1677), Pelham Humfrey (1647–1674) and John Blow (1649–1708). Each wrote music for the theatre as well as songs, anthems and instrumental works, and influenced the greatest composer of the English Restoration period—Henry Purcell (1659–1695). Purcell was organist of Westminster Abbey and to the Chapel Royal—a musical institution, not a building—and the holder of several other royal appointments. He responded to the tastes and fashions favoured by the king with music for various theatrical productions. He also composed the first true English opera, *Dido and Aeneas*, which is not only of historical interest, but contains some of the most beautiful music written by an English composer.

Jean-Philippe Rameau (1683–1746) was the next great composer of operas in France after Lully. He served the French taste for spectacle with very imaginative music to accompany such stage effects as earthquakes, thunderstorms or the appearance of terrible monsters, and thought of new ways of increasing the pace and excitement of opera. But Rameau did not start writing operas until fairly late in life. Earlier he had been a noted composer of music for the harpsichord and other keyboard instruments.

This was another field of music in which French composers of the baroque period played an important part. François Couperin (1668–1733) was the outstanding keyboard composer of his time and place. Couperin *le Grand* ('The Great'), as he was known in order to distinguish him from the other talented members of his musical family, also held a post at Louis XIV's court where he was in great demand as a teacher. He gave descriptive or fanciful titles to many of his compositions, such as *Les Petits Moulins à Vent* ('The Little Windmills') and *Le Rossignol en Amour* ('The Nightingale in Love'), to please his young pupils, and also to show the special connection that could exist between the image conjured up by the words and the music itself. Two hundred years later Debussy, another great French composer of keyboard music, explored such a connection in greater depth. Couperin wrote a treatise called *L'Art de toucher le clavecin* ('The Art of Playing the Harpsichord') which musical scholars find most valuable in their attempts to discover exactly how keyboard music was played in Couperin's own day. The whole question of changing styles of performance from one period to another, and of looking beyond the actual notes of a piece of music to the way they might have been played at the time they were first written down, is one which interests many musicians.

Most of Couperin's pieces were published in groups, originally called *ordres*, but better known today as suites. The word *suite* is itself French, meaning 'a following' in the sense of a succession of pieces. In the 19th and 20th centuries, the word suite has often been used to describe a selection of melodies taken from a much larger work like an opera or ballet. But as Couperin and his contemporaries knew it, the suite comprised a group of keyboard pieces usually based on the court dances of the time, like the *allemande, bourrée, courante, forlane, gavotte, gigue, minuet, rigaudon* and *sarabande*. Even when composers of other nationalities wrote suites they usually retained these French titles.

The other kind of instrumental music for which the baroque period is famous was that written for the stringed instruments of the violin family. Violins began to be made in the 16th century. They had tighter strings, were played with a stiffer bow, and were generally designed both to produce a clearer, brighter tone and to lend themselves to more intricate manipulation than the older viols. But viols in consort were best for playing the polyphonic music of renaissance times, and composers did not take violins very seriously until there were changes in musical tastes and styles.

Violins (from the Italian *violino* or 'small viola'), and their deeper toned relatives, violas, cellos (*violoncello* or 'small violone') and double basses (*violone* or 'great viola'), really began to supersede viols during the 17th century—a process that was encouraged by improvements in their design and structure. In this connection the little north Italian town of Cremona gained lasting fame by being the place where several families of instrument makers lived and worked. Violins, violas and cellos made by such celebrated members of these families as Nicolo Amati, Giuseppe Guaneri and Antonio Stradivari are now among the most highly prized possessions in the world of music—though few of these instruments have survived in their original form. They were nearly all modified during the 19th century, when other big changes were made in violin design (together with changes in playing styles).

Italian composers were also among the first to exploit the qualities of the violin family of instruments, writing for them music of an exciting new brilliance and vigour. In the process they created new musical forms. Arcangelo Corelli (1653–1713), Giuseppe Torelli (1658–1709), Tomaso Albinoni (1671–1750) and Francesco Geminiani (1687–1762) are noted for their compositions in the form of the concerto grosso or 'great concerto'. The Italian word *concerto* literally means 'agreement'. As Corelli and his contemporaries used the word, it described a composition for a sizeable group of string players whose parts followed an 'agreed' pattern. This pattern or style often involved the division of the players into a large group and a small group, to provide interesting contrasts of tone in an antiphonal way.

The recognised master of composition for stringed instruments in the concerto grosso style was Antonio Vivaldi (about

Two 18th century drawings, of a prompter at the opera (left) and a cellist

1685–1741), whose best known work has the descriptive title *Le Quattro Stagioni* ('The Four Seasons'). Vivaldi was for many years in charge of music at a school in Venice. He was also a priest, and because of the colour of his hair, was known as the 'red priest'. He wrote nearly five hundred works of various kinds for stringed instruments, as well as operas, oratorios and large quantities of church music. This prodigious output is typical of many 17th and 18th century composers. They nearly all held some church or court appointment, and in either case were expected to produce a new piece of music for all occasions. Many pieces were probably performed only once in a composer's lifetime, the music then being put aside and perhaps lost altogether. For this reason it is not unusual for musical scholars to re-discover pieces by 17th and 18th century composers, which have probably lain, in their original manuscript form, in some church, library or house, gathering dust for two or three hundred years. Sometimes it is difficult for scholars to identify the actual composer, because most composers of that time shared the same conventions of musical style so that much of their music has a very similar character. In addition, they frequently made arrangements of each other's work.

Another musical form whose beginnings are closely associated with the violin is the sonata. This word, taken from the Italian *suonare* ('to sound'), is applied to instrumental compositions of various kinds, in the way that a cantata, from the word *cantare* ('to sing'), describes a piece for voices. Early sonatas, written for small groups of stringed instruments with a keyboard accompaniment, were called *sonata da chiesa* if they were intended for performance in church, and *sonata da camera* if they were to be played in a room. Giuseppe Tartini (1692–1770) composed many sonatas for solo violin and accompanying keyboard instrument, so helping to establish one of the best-known types of sonata composition. Tartini was a famous violinist—'he does not play the violin but sings upon it,' was how one of his friends described his playing— and made some notable improvements to the instrument, especially to the construction of the bow. His best known work today is the so-called 'Devil's Trill' Sonata, inspired, according to Tartini himself, by a dream in which he heard the Devil play the violin.

Throughout the renaissance and baroque periods Italy was the musical centre of Europe. Most new musical ideas and techniques originated from there, and it was during this time that the use of the Italian language for musical terms and expressions became widespread. France, too, was an important and influential country in musical affairs as it was in philosophy and politics. Germany, still consisting of many separate states and principalities from the time of the Holy Roman Empire, was considered a very provincial part of Europe by comparison, and even in their own country German musicians often had to take second place to Italians or Frenchmen over the matter of court appointments. All this was soon to change. The two composers who are now recognised as the greatest masters of the baroque period were both Germans, and they mark the beginning of a long period during which the world of music was dominated by German or German-speaking musicians.

One of these composers was Georg Friedrich Händel

(1685–1759). Opera appealed to him early in his career, and after a period in Hamburg where his first two operas were produced, he went to Italy to study the orchestral music of Corelli and the operas of Alessandro Scarlatti (1660–1725). This composer worked chiefly in Naples and created a style of *opera seria*—'serious opera'—which was very influential in the early 18th century, not least with Händel himself.

The growing popularity of Italian opera in England then attracted Händel to London, which was fast becoming the richest city in Europe due to the maritime trade between Britain, America and the East under the protection of the British navy. Händel was welcomed in England, adopted British nationality and modified his name to George Frideric Handel—the odd spelling of 'Frideric' rather than 'Frederick' being due to the composer's unfamiliarity with the English language. One person who was pleased to employ him was the Duke of Chandos, a businessman and profiteer involved at one time in the South Sea Bubble, an 18th century financial scandal to do with the opening up of new trade routes to the East. His estate was at Edgware, north of London, which the composer frequently visited for a time, writing for him a splendid group of anthems. But Handel's main ambition remained to compose opera for the London stage.

Opera has always been a tough challenge to composers because of the delicate balance it must try to maintain between music and drama; also because it is very expensive to produce, while at the mercy of all kinds of public whims and fancies. Handel had the temperament to cope with these problems and pressures, and composed nearly forty operas for the London stage, including *Rinaldo*, his first success, *Berenice* and *Xerxes*, from which comes the famous 'Largo'. Luck was also on his side, as when his earlier patron in Germany, the Elector of Hanover, became George I of England and gave him re-newed royal support. But he could not prevent changes in public taste, and such a change took place with the production of *The Beggar's Opera* by John Gay. This had English words, set to traditional English ballads and folk tunes, and London audiences found it a refreshing contrast to Italian *opera seria* which, apart from the question of language, was filled with rigid conventions about how many vocal parts there should be, how many arias each should be allotted, and when each singer

A fanciful picture of the London river scene in Handel's day. The gondola symbolises the popularity of Italian opera when Handel first arrived in England

should enter and leave the stage. This was the style of opera at which Handel excelled, and however beautiful his own music might be, it was a style that was suddenly losing its appeal with the British public. In addition, the pressures of work, commercial rivalries and artistic squabbles had finally made Handel ill. So, after a period of convalescence, he began to turn away from opera and to give more attention to oratorio.

Oratorio is a kind of religious opera, with vocal solos and choruses, but without stage sets or costumes. Its name is derived from the Oratory (a kind of chapel) of St Philip Neri in Rome, where the first oratorios were probably performed. An early master of oratorio was the Italian composer Giacomo Carissimi (1605–1674). Handel created an oratorio style specially suited to English tastes, writing some of his best music for the chorus. He also took advantage of the fact that oratorio could be performed during Lent, when opera was banned. After some setbacks and disappointments he achieved a new success with such oratorios as *Saul, Israel in Egypt* and, above all, *Messiah*. This work contains the 'Hallelujah Chorus', which brought George II reverently to his feet at the first performance in Dublin in 1742. From then on Handel's position in English society was secure, and he died a prosperous man. For a long time after Handel's death, performances of *Messiah* were given with increasingly large choruses and orchestras, and treated with great solemnity. Performances of it with the relatively small chorus and orchestra of Handel's own time reveal it as a bright and robust masterpiece of baroque choral music.

A feature of oratorio under Handel's own direction was a performance, during the interval, of one of his organ concertos, with himself as soloist. These concertos, his concerti grossi, the music he wrote for two public occasions—the *Water Music* and *Music for the Royal Fireworks*—and instrumental pieces like the theme with variations, nicknamed 'The Harmonious Blacksmith', also reflect the strong and resilient character of their composer. Handel had a habit of borrowing other composers' material when it suited him, but the sturdy spirit of the music is always his own.

The other German master of the baroque was Johann Sebastian Bach (1685–1750). He and Handel were born in the same year, within a hundred miles of each other—Handel in Halle, Bach in

Eisenach, both now in East Germany—and each of them went blind towards the end of their lives. But as people they were quite different, and so was the pattern of their lives. Bach never travelled outside Germany. He remained all his life a devoted family man, soon marrying again when his first wife died, and fathering twenty children. He held a series of posts as court musician or as organist and choirmaster, the last and most important of these being as Cantor (Director of Music) to St Thomas's church and school in Leipzig. To some extent Bach was given recognition, especially as an organist. He was once invited to the court at Potsdam by Frederick the Great of Prussia, who was a noted patron of music. But generally he remained in a position of comparative obscurity, far from cosmopolitan centres like London and Paris, where Handel sought fame and fortune.

One of Bach's most numerous group of works—nearly three hundred of them—are his church cantatas, written as a regular part of his duties for performance on different Sundays in the church year. Bach lived and worked in that part of Germany that was firmly Lutheran in its religion, so these cantatas, with orchestral accompaniment, are set to words in German. Some are elaborate compositions, with parts for several soloists and chorus. Others are much shorter and simpler, with a part for one or two soloists only. The piece known as 'Jesu, Joy of Man's Desiring' is taken from Cantata no. 147.

Bach's three largest choral compositions are his Mass in B minor, written in order to secure a court appointment, and his two oratorio-like settings of the Passion, both also written for special occasions, the *St John Passion* and *St Matthew Passion*. The Passion of Christ is that sequence of events leading to His crucifixion, as told in the four New Testament gospels, and musical settings of the Passion story, using elements of plainsong and simple polyphony, date from the Middle Ages. The unique drama of the Passion was always keenly felt, and at the words, relating to the actual moment of Christ's death upon the cross, 'And behold, the veil of the temple was rent in twain from the top to the bottom' (St Matthew's Gospel), there was a tradition for the priest actually to rend a cloth during a hushed and dramatic pause in the musical recitation.

Bach's *St John* and *St Matthew Passions* were largely modelled on

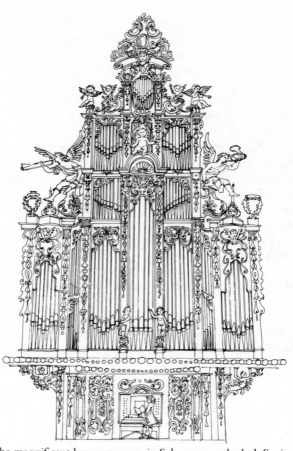

The magnificent baroque organ in Salamanca cathedral, Spain

the four Passions of Heinrich Schütz (1585–1672), an earlier German composer who had studied with Giovanni Gabrieli and Monteverdi in Venice and learnt from them a dramatic style of choral and vocal writing, which included the antiphonal use of voices. Like Bach's church cantatas, they were written for the Lutheran church and so use the German Bible, with a chorus and solo parts for Christ himself, Judas and Pontius Pilate. Bach incorporated into both his Passions a melody by another important German predecessor, Hans Leo Hassler (1564–1612), and also the great Lutheran chorales which add even more to the music's sense of a deep and unshakeable faith.

Bach's second great group of works are those for the organ. There had been several eminent organist-composers before Bach. One was the Italian Girolamo Frescobaldi (1583–1643). As organist at St Peter's, Rome, thousands gathered to hear him play. There were other fine organists in Italy, France and England, but during the baroque period an especially strong tradition of organ music grew up in Germany and the Low Countries (Holland and Belgium). Frescobaldi himself was for some years organist at Antwerp cathedral. Jan Pieterszoon Sweelinck (1562–1611) was a Dutchman who pioneered new organ techniques, and was the teacher of many other Dutch and German organist-composers. Diderik (or Dietrich) Buxtehude (1637–1707) was Danish, but spent most of his career as organist at the German Baltic port of Lübeck. As a young man Bach once walked two hundred miles to Lübeck to hear Buxtehude play. There were also great German organ builders like Gottfried Silbermann—a Saxon builder well known to Bach. The instruments they made were usually designed as a major embellishment to the church or palace for which they were intended. During the 19th century organs increased greatly in size and power, but many modern organs are again constructed along the lines of the instruments of Bach's day.

Bach continued in this tradition with organ works in every established form: fantasias, being fairly free expressions of a musical idea; toccatas, from the Italian verb *toccare* ('To touch'), and intended primarily as pieces to display finger control; chorale-preludes, based on existing Lutheran chorale tunes; and preludes and fugues. The fugue is the most developed form of polyphonic music. A theme is first played, or stated, on its own, then built upon itself, sometimes in combination with other themes, according to various sets of rules. An analysis of fugal composition may seem severe and academic. Even the word has a forbidding sound to it. But fugues themselves can achieve a strength and power which has no equal in any other kind of music.

Bach was the consummate master of this form, and also wrote fugues for other instruments. For the harpsichord he composed a monumental set of Forty-eight Preludes and Fugues. The number is significant. There is one prelude and one corresponding fugue for each of the twenty-four major and minor scales. The change from the medieval system of church modes to this new arrangement of scales, all harmonically related, took place during the renaissance period. The *key* (an indication of the scale) in which a piece was written, and the way in which the music could move harmonically, or *modulate*, from one key to another, became a matter of increasing importance to composers. Bach's Forty-eight Preludes and Fugues were intended to promote a new method of tuning keyboard instruments which could accommodate equally well music written in any of the twenty-four major and minor scales. Hence the other name for them is *Das wohltemperierte Clavier* ('The Well-Tempered Clavier', in other words, a well-tuned keyboard). They are a prime example of how a composer of genius can transform a technical exercise into a great work of art.

Besides the Forty-eight Preludes and Fugues, Bach composed a large amount of instrumental and orchestral music, including the so-called 'Goldberg Variations', written for a pupil named Goldberg, whose patron wanted music to help him sleep; numerous suites (or partitas); and six orchestral works in the concerto grosso style, each requiring a different combination of instruments, dedicated to the Margrave (or Count) of Brandenburg, and called the Brandenburg Concertos. Bach had disappointments in his life, and he could be a very stubborn man when he disagreed with his various employers. But much of this music, written for private entertainment rather than public performance, is genial and relaxed, as well as being full of great musical ideas.

Handel and Bach were two of the last composers of the baroque period. The grand scale of much of their choral music, and the contrapuntal forms, like the fugue, which they frequently used, were passing out of fashion while they were still alive. Bach, especially, was soon regarded as a very old-fashioned composer, not least by his own sons, and his music was neglected for nearly a century after his death. The new musical fashion corresponded to a style of art and decoration called rococo. This was characterised by delicate ornamentation, intended to charm rather than to impress or inspire. The French artist Jean-Antoine Watteau was a master of this rococo style, and the delicacy and elegance of his work is in marked contrast to the often massive and opulent paintings of an earlier baroque artist like Peter Paul Rubens.

Couperin and Rameau, contemporaries of Bach, had already cultivated a similarly light and decorative style in their keyboard music, sometimes called the *style galant*. In Germany Georg Philipp Telemann (1681–1767) was born four years earlier than Handel and Bach and outlived them both. He wrote numerous operas, oratorios and vast quantities of instrumental music, and in the process also helped to bring about a change from the baroque style to the much lighter and more graceful rococo style.

Rococo art was a sign that after a long period of religious and political strife, going back to the time of the Reformation, Europe was settling down to a period of comparative peace. Rococo decoration and music were an expression of people's desire to relax and enjoy art without having to take it too seriously.

A more significant attitude of mind which grew up during the 18th century was concerned with the ideal of Reason. Philosophers and educated people in general believed that through their own powers of reason they could bring peace and order to civilisation and to the natural world about them. They greatly admired the beauty of such monuments of classical antiquity as the Parthenon in Athens, which many of them saw on their tours of Europe. In their eyes a building like the Parthenon perfectly expressed the principles of order and proportion. The new 18th century style of architecture and design, called neo-classical, or new classical, embodied many of these features; and the whole artistic movement of the time is now called the classical period.

The classical period in music lasted from about the middle to the end of the 18th century. Musicians of the period were equally interested in matters of order and proportion, and created new musical forms and styles through which to express them.

A beautifully decorated two-manual harpsichord of the rococo period

One of these forms was the symphony. The word symphony, meaning 'a sounding together', had been used by earlier composers to describe an orchestral interlude in a larger choral work, such as the so-called 'Pastoral' Symphony in Handel's *Messiah*. But the symphony, as people think of it today, was a type of composition that dates from the classical period. It developed from the kind of Italian operatic overture (or *sinfonia*) which had a fast opening section, a slow middle section and a fast closing section (as distinct from the type of French overture created by Lully). This fast-slow-fast arrangement offered composers a satisfying sense of form and balance, and quite soon they were writing symphonies that divided these sections up into separate pieces, or movements, contained within the structure of the whole. For some time also, such works were often still described as 'grand overtures'.

The most carefully worked out musical representation of these classical ideals of form and proportion was a special way of constructing a single piece of music, called *sonata form*. A composer who helped to lay the foundations of sonata form was Alessandro Scarlatti's son, Domenico Scarlatti (1685–1757), who held an appointment with the Spanish royal court in Madrid for many years. Domenico Scarlatti is best remembered today for his hundreds of keyboard sonatas. In these single-movement compositions he achieved a good sense of balance and form by modulating the music from one key to another suitably related key and then modulating back to the original key again. This was called two-part form, or *binary form*, and sonata form grew out of it.

In sonata form a piece of music is divided into three principal sections, called exposition, development and recapitulation. Within these sections there are further subdivisions relating to the presentation of two contrasting themes, the passages linking them, and also linking the different sections together. Strict sonata form presented composers with many new rules, especially over matters of harmonic modulation and key relationships. At the same time, it allowed them to introduce far more ideas into a single piece of music than had been possible before.

The kinds of themes composers used in sonata form were usually quite different from those found in earlier types of music. They were much shorter so that they should fit comfortably into the larger structure of the whole movement. At the same time they were constructed in such a way that they could easily be 'taken apart' for the purposes of development and 'reassembled' for the recapitulation. Beyond that composers were concerned with questions of musical contrast, as between the character or mood of the themes to be used, the keys to be played in, and between soft and loud passages serving to underline the structure of the music.

Musicians experimented a good deal with these new ideas and forms at the court of Mannheim in Germany, and a composer who took a leading part in the process was Jan Stamic (1717–1757) from that part of central Europe which is now Czechoslovakia. Jan Stamic, or Johann Stamitz to give the more usual German version of his name, was *kapellmeister* (musical director) to the court, which maintained a good orchestra. The numerous states and principalities which made up Germany often used to exchange musicians for their orchestras and choirs in much the same way that football clubs transfer players today, and the court of Mannheim had acquired some of the best musicians of the time. Stamitz and his colleagues formed what is known as the Mannheim School, and together they developed many new ways of writing orchestral music.

They devoted much time and thought to the sound qualities and abilities of each instrument, or group of instruments, and how these could best be combined to produce a clear, well balanced orchestral sound. One of their achievements was the creation of an effective contrast between soft and loud passages of music. Such loud passages, using the full orchestra, in contrast to passages for a few instruments only, are described by the word *tutti*, the Italian word for 'all'. Another achievement of the Mannheim School was the orchestral *crescendo*—a carefully controlled build-up of orchestral sound from soft to loud. At the same time they abandoned certain orchestral practices of the earlier baroque period, such as the writing of high-pitched trumpet parts, called clarino trumpet parts. Clarino trumpet players in the time of Bach and Handel were much sought after and highly paid for their special skills. But this type of playing was too florid and intrusive for the well-ordered kind of orchestral sound the Mannheim musicians were striving to attain.

Johann Stamitz himself wrote about fifty symphonies, including in some of them parts for the clarinet which was a relatively new woodwind instrument and not much used before his time. The Italian Giovanni Battista Sammartini (1698–1775) was another early and influential composer of symphonies, although he had no direct connection with the Mannheim musicians. Sammartini was one of Gluck's teachers, and Gluck himself (discussed later) had many new ideas about orchestration as applied to opera.

The kind of *dynamics*—degrees of softness and loudness—used by the early composers of symphonies, also became possible in the writing of keyboard music, following the invention, early in the 18th century, of the piano. What made the piano different from existing keyboard instruments was a mechanism by which a hammer struck the string of the note and bounced straight off again, allowing the string to continue vibrating, thus producing a sound of greater volume and subject to greater control.

The probable inventor of this clever device (as in the case of many inventions and discoveries there were several people working on the idea at about the same time) was the Italian craftsman Bartolommeo Cristofori. The instrument he designed which made use of it he called the *gravicembalo col piano e forte*—'harpsichord with soft and loud'. In practice, early pianofortes were not very different from other keyboard instruments, but they were steadily improved to give much stronger sound and also to give the player a finer range of dynamics, so that by the end of the 18th century they had virtually displaced older keyboard instruments like the harpsichord and clavichord.

Two important composers of the new style of keyboard music were sons of J. S. Bach. Carl Philipp Emanuel Bach (1714–1788), who was for some years employed at the court of King Frederick the Great of Prussia at Potsdam, near Berlin, composed many keyboard sonatas which are of great interest for the way they mark the change in style from writing for the harpsichord to writing for the piano. C. P. E. Bach also wrote symphonies and other works in the new classical style quite different in character from the music of his father. Johann Christian Bach (1735–1782) is known as the 'English Bach' or 'London Bach' because after a time in Italy he settled in the British capital and was employed in the royal household of George III. J. C. Bach wrote a number of keyboard concertos which are interesting forerunners of the concerto style as developed by Mozart. In fact, he gave some instruction to Mozart, when the latter visited London as a child.

However, the man who most completely sums up the achievements of the classical period was Franz Joseph Haydn (1732–1809). He was born in the village of Rohrau, which is now in eastern Austria, bordering on Hungary, and for much of his career was *kapellmeister* to the aristocratic Esterhazy family from the Hungarian district of Galanta. As a normal part of his duties Haydn composed masses, oratorios, operas; and towards the end of his life he wrote his two most famous oratorios, *The Creation* and *The Seasons*. Haydn's principal patron and employer for many years was Prince Nikolaus Esterhazy, a cultured man who was as close to being the composer's friend as the relationship between master and servant would allow. He gave Haydn plenty of opportunity to experiment with the new instrumental and orchestral styles, and it is for his work in these fields that Haydn is chiefly remembered today.

Haydn wrote keyboard sonatas, usually with three movements. The general rule for these movements was to have the first written in sonata form, and taken at a moderately fast speed; the second movement to be a theme with variations written upon it, and

Haydn and his friends rehearse a new string quartet. In his day chamber music was often written with particular players in mind

taken fairly slowly; and the third movement to be in the form of a rondo, this consisting of a main theme repeated several times over with other themes placed between each repetition, to be taken at a brisk tempo in order to round the whole work off with a nicely calculated flourish.

He wrote instrumental trios for piano, violin and cello, based on much the same arrangement of three movements. And he perfected, over many years, the art of string quartet composition. The classical string quartet consisted of two violins, a viola and a cello, a beautifully balanced combination of stringed instruments, allowing the music for each instrument to be heard very clearly in relation to the rest. For his quartets, Haydn usually included four movements, the third of these being in the form of a minuet (inherited from the older suite) with a middle section called a trio, because such pieces were originally written with three independent parts. One of the best known of Haydn's quartets is the Quartet in C major (opus 76 no. 3), containing a theme called the 'Emperor's

Hymn', which Haydn had previously composed. In later times the German Empire took the tune over, and it is still used for the national anthem of the German Federal Republic. In the 'Emperor' Quartet it is used as the basis for a set of variations.

By tradition, music for any small group of instruments is called 'chamber music', which in the 18th century meant music intended for performance in a room rather than a larger concert hall or church. In Haydn's time most chamber music was also written with particular performers in mind, and it is easy to imagine the pleasure with which Haydn and other musicians attached to the court must often have tried out his latest trio or quartet in the rooms assigned to them.

Above all, Haydn is associated with the symphony. He wrote more than the 104 symphonies with which he is officially credited, and in them he consolidated upon the work of the Mannheim school and other symphonists of the time. He divided his orchestra up into four principal groups, or 'families', of instruments—strings, woodwind, brass and percussion—giving to each a clearly defined role in the balance of orchestral sound. He was only writing for an orchestra of about thirty-five players, but this basic selection and classification of instruments—the result of years of trial and error—has lasted until the present day. Haydn also accepted the four-movement plan as the standard pattern for the symphony, very similar to that which he adopted for the string quartet.

Some of Haydn's best known symphonies are among the twelve he composed for his two visits to England, when he was already a famous man. They are symphonies nos 93 to 104, and are known as the 'Salomon Symphonies', after the violinist and impresario J. P. Salomon, who sponsored the visits. Most of them have nicknames. Symphony no. 94 in G major is called the 'Surprise' Symphony. This has a loud chord which unexpectedly interrupts the quiet progress of the slow movement. Haydn had a lively sense of humour, and audiences today can still be caught off guard by this famous chord.

Such wit and sparkle, combined with a mastery of form and style, are the hallmark of all Haydn's mature symphonies. They are the music of a brilliant man who also enjoyed a long, successful and, on the whole, happy life. They are also the foundation upon

49

which Beethoven, Schubert, Brahms, Bruckner, Mahler and others could build up the symphony into the most elevated kind of orchestral composition.

Wolfgang Amadeus Mozart (1756–1791) is the other great composer of the classical period. Mozart was twenty-four years younger than Haydn, and, had he lived as long as the older man would have survived well into the period of 19th century romantic art. This is an interesting point to make, because in several significant ways Mozart did anticipate social and artistic changes in the 19th century, although he did not live long enough to be a part of them.

Mozart was an infant prodigy. He was able to play the harpsichord at about the age of four, and was writing little pieces of music before he was seven. His father, Leopold, took Wolfgang and his sister on tours round the courts of Europe, including London. They received many gifts from the kings and queens, dukes and duchesses whom they astonished and delighted with their playing.

After this glittering start to his career, however, things did not go well for Mozart. As a young man he entered the service of Count Hieronymous Colloredo, Archbishop of Salzburg (where Haydn's talented brother Michael also held an appointment). Salzburg was Mozart's birthplace, but after his earlier travels he found it a very dull place. In addition, Archbishop Hieronymous was not very musical, and Mozart came to detest him. 'I hate the Archbishop almost to a fury,' he wrote to his father. Soon after that he was dismissed from his post. He never obtained another worthwhile position, nor received the support of a really sympathetic patron. Some of his operas were big successes, but there were no copyright laws to protect his interests, and he did not have the business sense, toughness or luck of a composer like Handel. Consequently he and his family became almost destitute, and when he died his body was thrown into a pauper's mass grave.

The extraordinary fact about Mozart is that as his personal situation grew worse, so his creative powers grew ever stronger. Throughout his career he wrote serenades, divertimenti and sets of dances on commission. The well known serenade, *Eine Kleine Nachtsmusik* ('A Little Night Music', K 525), is an example of how brilliantly he could write this kind of 'occasional' music. But during the last six or seven years of his life, when his situation was often quite desperate, a beauty and expressive richness were added to the flawless musical craftsmanship he always displayed. Some of Mozart's most serene music was written at moments of acute despair or anxiety, and no more remarkable example can be found of the ability of many great artists to separate completely their inner creative life from the outward circumstances of their existence.

The great compositions of these last six or seven years can most easily be identified by their 'K' number. Over six hundred works were later catalogued and placed in their probable order of composition by a scholar named Ludwig von Köchel, and today they are invariably quoted with their Köchel, or 'K' number. With a few exceptions, it is the works with 'K' numbers above 400 which contain Mozart's greatest music. These include the string quartets in D minor (K421) and in C major (K467, known as the 'Dissonance' Quartet), which are two from the set of six Mozart dedicated to his friend Haydn; the string quintets in C major (K515), in G minor (K516) and in D major (K593); and the last three symphonies. These are symphonies no. 39 in E flat major (K543); no. 40 in G minor (K550); and no. 41 in C major (K551), called the 'Jupiter' Symphony. Apparently these last three symphonies were not commissioned, but were written on impulse, in the space of six or seven weeks. To compose in this way, in response to some purely personal compulsion, was to be a fairly common practice among 19th century romantic composers and artists in general, but was still most unusual in the classical world of the 18th century to which Mozart belonged. These symphonies look dramatically forward in other ways also. Each has a mood and character which gives it great individuality, and there are passages—as there are in some of Mozart's other mature works—where his creative thinking seems to lead him quite instinctively towards the kind of harmonic 'chromaticism' developed by Wagner and others nearly a century later.

The other group of Mozart's orchestral works, written specially for himself as the soloist, and which are significant for the way they look forward in time, are his piano concertos. A notable feature of them is the way Mozart shares out the music between the orchestra and the solo instrument, and there are many passages which sound very like a conversation between the piano and various instruments of the orchestra. Indeed, 'dialogue' is a word that is often used to describe concerto writing of this sort. With his piano concertos, Mozart left right behind the style of the old concerto grosso, and in such of them as the D minor (K466), C minor (K491) and C major (K503) concertos, he also wrote music which opens the way to the dramatic power and scale of Beethoven.

Another of their features is the *cadenza*. This is the Italian word for 'cadence', which in music is a kind of harmonic punctuation mark, usually consisting of two chords. In classical cadenzas, two chords bring the flow of the music to a temporary halt, so that the soloist can play a passage of music entirely on his own, intended to display his skills. In Mozart's time the soloist would have been expected to extemporise upon the themes already heard in the movement. But today a pianist or other concerto soloist almost always prepares his cadenzas in advance; and, starting with Beethoven, composers themselves usually wrote their own cadenzas, working them more and more closely into the overall structure of the music.

Among Mozart's other concertos for various instruments is the Clarinet Concerto in A major (K622). This concerto belongs to a small group of works which Mozart specially composed for a clarinetist named Anton Stadler. They are a notable example of the way in which composers have often been inspired by the playing or singing of a particular artist.

Mozart wrote for the voice with the same love and understanding as he did for instruments. Some of his best early music was vocal, like the motet *Exsultate, jubilate* (K165); while his last, unfinished composition was a Requiem Mass (K626), completed by his pupil Franz Süssmayr. Greatest of all is the vocal music of his operas.

Vienna, where Mozart lived for much of his adult life, was then the capital city of the Habsburg Empire, which covered much of the territory of present-day Austria, Czechoslovakia and Hungary. It was a lively, colourful city, filled with people of many different races from central and eastern Europe. The influence of eastern Europe extended to the Ottoman, or Turkish Empire, which had been a threat to Christian Europe ever since the Fall of Constantinople in 1453. Vienna itself had been threatened by Turkish forces as late as 1683. A hundred years after, there remained a fashionable Viennese interest in Turkish art and culture. This formed the basis for Mozart's relatively early opera *Die Entführung aus dem Serail* ('The Abduction from the Harem', K384), also known by the Italian title *Il Seraglio*. The plot of the opera is quite trivial, but what makes it such a fine work are the joyous high spirits of much of the music (including mock-Turkish effects), and the real feeling for the characters that Mozart conveys through some of their arias.

Mozart's wonderful response to stage situations, and his ability to portray characters as real people, reached its peak in his collaboration with the Italian librettist Lorenzo da Ponte. The first fruit of this collaboration was *Le Nozze di Figaro* ('The Marriage of Figaro', K492). It is described as *opera buffa*, a type of Italian comic opera which had been made very successful earlier in the 18th century by Giovanni Battista Pergolesi (1710–1736). But through a succession of the most beautiful and expressive arias Mozart invests his characters with a degree of feeling that carries the opera far beyond the bounds of comedy. *Le Nozze di Figaro* is also remarkable for its social realism. When the curtain rises at the end of the overture, instead of a scene of opulence, or a group of idealised characters from history or mythology, there is Figaro on his knees, measuring the space needed for his marriage bed. A little later he sings, with reference to his master, the Count of Almaviva, 'If you want to dance, then you shall—but to *my* tune!' The suggestion that a servant might get the better of his aristocratic master was still very daring in 1786, when the opera was first produced. The play by Pierre-Augustin de Beaumarchais, on which the opera was based, had already caused trouble in France, where it was seen as an attack on the existing social order.

Don Giovanni being cast into Hell

Mozart's second operatic masterpiece, with da Ponte as his librettist, was *Don Giovanni* (K527), based on the life of the legendary Spanish lover and adventurer, Don Juan. In the course of the opera the wicked Don Giovanni mocks the statue erected to a man whom he has killed in a fight. The statue comes to life, arrives at the Don's palace and has him thrown into hell. The way towards such dramatic realism in opera had been opened up by the German composer Christoph Willibald Gluck (1714–1787). He was one of the great reforming figures in the history of opera, arguing that conventions over matters of singing or staging should not be allowed to hinder the progress of the plot or stand in the way of any dramatic situation. Da Ponte's libretto and Mozart's music combine to make *Don Giovanni* one of the most dramatically effective of all operas. The overture plays its part in this with a slow introduction which looks forward to the spine-chilling events of the last scene. After Mozart composers generally gave more time and thought to overtures, often including in them themes from the operas themselves and so giving them more significance.

Così fan tutte (K588) is the third opera by Mozart and da Ponte. The title is hardly ever translated, but it can be taken to mean 'Women Are All The Same', and this sums up the light-hearted character of the work. At one point it makes fun of the 'animal magnetism' ideas of Dr Franz Mesmer which were all the rage in fashionable society at the time.

With his opera *Die Zauberflöte* ('The Magic Flute', K620), Mozart returned to a German libretto, and to the style known as *Singspiel*, which he had used in *Die Entführung aus dem Serail*. The Italian operatic practice of recitative and aria required the dialogue between the arias or vocal ensembles to be sung. In *Singspiel* ('sing-play') the dialogue was spoken, as in an ordinary play. Its use by Mozart and other German-speaking composers of the time marked the beginnings of a German style of opera, quite distinct from the Italian and French operatic styles. The routine of spoken dialogue between set songs, choruses, or numbers, has also been continued in operetta and most 20th century stage musicals.

Die Zauberflöte is an extraordinary work. It is set in an ancient kingdom on the banks of the Nile, and is based on a kind of fairy tale, with characters like the Queen of the Night and Papageno the Bird-catcher. There is also a monster, magic bells and the magic flute itself. At the same time, it presents much of the symbolism and ritual of Freemasonary (of which society Mozart was a member), and expresses such ideals as the nobility and brotherhood of man. When Mozart was setting these ideals to music in the last year of his life, the Bastille in Paris had already fallen and the French Revolution had begun.

Ludwig van Beethoven (1770–1827) was still a young man when the French Revolution started. He believed passionately in the revolutionary slogan of *Liberté, Egalité, Fraternité*—'Liberty, Equality, Brotherhood'—and in several of his greatest works he openly expressed these ideals. His only opera *Fidelio* is about people imprisoned for their beliefs and their eventual release in the name of liberty and justice. His 'Choral' Symphony is so named because of the chorus in the last movement, which sets to music a poem called *Ode to Joy* by the poet Johann Schiller, proclaiming that men and women everywhere are all equal in the Brotherhood of Man. The same kind of idealism made Beethoven angrily withdraw the dedication of his *Eroica* Symphony to Napoleon, when he heard that Napoleon had had himself crowned Emperor of the French. To Beethoven this was a betrayal of the Revolution, which had earlier done away with the monarchy in France.

The French Revolution and the Napoleonic Wars which followed had a profound effect on the life and times of Beethoven and others of his generation. The settled order of 18th century life was destroyed by these events, and this changed the whole climate of philosophical and artistic thought. Instead of the idea of order and harmony between man and nature, which had lain behind so much 18th century music and painting, there was the notion of man battling to find his destiny in a hostile universe. 'I will seize fate by the throat' was one of Beethoven's most celebrated sayings, and the whole pattern of his life and art was one of constant struggle. It is remarkable, in this context, that he, among all the great composers, was the one to go deaf—the worst thing that could happen to a musician. This put an end to his career as a composer-pianist, and made it virtually impossible for him to hold any other official appointment. Beethoven did have generous and enlightened patrons who recognised his genius and helped to support him. But the affliction of deafness, his aims as an artist and his own attempts to pay his way in the world could have broken a man without his great strength of will. In fact, Beethoven's efforts to assert himself, and his refusal to compromise where his work was concerned, did much to change the status of the artist in society.

Beethoven was born in the Rhineland town of Bonn (now capital of the German Federal Republic). At about the same time

Two studies of Beethoven. Wherever he went he carried a note book in which he could jot down ideas as they came to him

that he started to go deaf he settled permanently in Vienna, though his way of life remained hectic and unsettled to the end. He changed his lodgings on average twice a year, usually on account of a quarrel with his landlord. Many of the stories about Beethoven refer to his suspicion, impatience and bad temper in his dealings with other people. His deafness could account for some of this. But his eccentric and unpredictable behaviour must to a great extent have been caused by the inner struggle of his creative life. He dramatically enlarged the forms of music he inherited from Haydn, Mozart and other composers of the classical period, in order to encompass the power and intensity of his own feelings and ideas. These objectives presented Beethoven with enormous technical problems, and his music sometimes sounds as if it really is hammering its way through to a solution of them.

The more general quality of Beethoven's music is its strength and concentration. He left behind him a number of so-called sketch books, in which he jotted down ideas as they came to him. A study of these shows how he revised his ideas over and over again until at last they were ready to fit into a larger musical structure Beethoven's ability to make his ideas grow is strikingly demonstrated in the three successive overtures he wrote for early productions of his opera *Leonora*. The listener can hear for himself how Beethoven changed and enlarged upon his ideas from one overture to the next. For a later production of the opera, when its title had been changed to *Fidelio*, he wrote another and quite different overture. The effort of building up his ideas in this way also meant that Beethoven sometimes spent years working on a composition, as in the case of the Mass in D (*Missa Solemnis*, opus 123). The first performance of this work—one of Beethoven's largest—was planned for the installation of the composer's patron the Archduke Rudolph, as an Archbishop, but it was not finished until several years after the event.

Beethoven's best known orchestral compositions are his nine symphonies. As in the case of all his major groups of works, there is a constant sense of growth and change from one symphony to the next; a sense of reaching out all the time towards new goals. In this context, the opus numbers, which refer to the order of publication of individual works, or small groups of works, are of interest for the way they help to mark the progress of Beethoven's creative thinking. In only a few cases do these opus numbers fail to correspond to the general order of composition.

The fact that Beethoven wrote only nine symphonies, compared with the symphonic outputs of Haydn and Mozart, is another indication of the time and effort he put into his work. The First Symphony in C major (opus 21) still sounds quite like a symphony by Haydn, though there are some very original ideas in it. The Ninth Symphony in D minor ('Choral', opus 125) composed towards the end of Beethoven's life, is as far in advance of the earlier work as an oak tree is to an acorn. The intervening symphonies are all quite different in character from each other, and some have particularly noteworthy features. The first movement of the Fifth Symphony in C minor (opus 67) is the most celebrated example of Beethoven's genius for constructing a piece of music from the briefest of phrases. This opening phrase also acts as a 'motto theme' for the symphony as a whole, recurring in one form or another throughout the work, to give it a special unity. The

Sixth Symphony in F major (*Pastoral*, opus 68) is the first symphony with a 'programme'—in this case evocations of the countryside, inspired by Beethoven's love of the woods and fields around Vienna. Both these symphonies also break new ground by having some of their movements linked together. Beethoven also created the symphonic scherzo. *Scherzo* is the Italian for 'joke', but Beethoven used the word to describe a much speeded up and more dynamic version of the minuet which formed the third movement of most symphonies before his time. The first typical Beethoven scherzo, full of explosive bursts of energy, occurs in the Third Symphony in E flat major (*Eroica*, opus 55). The scherzo of the 'Choral' Symphony comes immediately after the first movement, thus reversing the usual order of the second and third movements in the established form of the 18th century classical symphony.

For the concert hall Beethoven also composed five piano concertos, a violin concerto, a 'triple' concerto for violin, cello and piano, and several powerful and dramatic overtures in addition to those he wrote for his opera *Fidelio*. After the symphonies, however, the other two most substantial groups of his compositions are the piano sonatas and string quartets.

Beethoven wrote more music for the piano, in one form or another, than for any other instrument. And despite his deafness, he remained aware of the technical improvements to the instrument which were made during his lifetime. In his thirty-two piano sonatas he tested to the limit the piano's growing capabilities. The Sonata in C sharp minor (opus 27, no. 2), popularly known as the 'Moonlight' Sonata; the Sonata in C major (opus 53), called the 'Waldstein' Sonata; and the Sonata in F minor (*Appassionata*, opus 57) are examples of Beethoven's dramatic piano style. The Sonata in B flat major (opus 106) is a very long and difficult piece, demanding great powers of concentration and stamina from the performer. It is called the 'Hammerklavier' Sonata. *Hammerklavier* is the German for 'piano' and, in fact, Beethoven applied the term to each of his last group of five piano sonatas.

In the 'Hammerklavier' Sonata itself, and in the sonatas in E major (opus 109) and C minor (opus 111) Beethoven included sets of variations on an original theme. Composers of the baroque and rococo periods had written sets of variations which usually stuck closely to the structure of the basic theme, in the way that a decorative artist might trace a series of patterns over the shape of an existing picture or design. Haydn and Mozart, in some of their variations, departed much further from the structure and character of the theme in question. Beethoven always saw the form of theme and variations as a challenge to his imagination and ingenuity, and used the theme itself as a mere starting point for his ideas, often producing variations far removed in structure and in spirit from that theme. One of his greatest piano works is the thirty-three variations he wrote on a waltz theme by the Viennese music publisher Antonio Diabelli (opus 120).

Beethoven originally wrote sixteen string quartets, but because one of his quartet movements was subsequently published as a composition on its own the total is usually given as seventeen. The six quartets published as his opus 18 contain some of the best music of his early creative period. The three quartets of opus 59 belong to what is called the composer's middle period, when he had reached full maturity as an artist. They are known as the 'Rassumovsky' quartets because they were commissioned by Count Andrei Rassumovsky, the Russian ambassador to Vienna and a keen amateur cellist. A story about them highlights another side of Beethoven's view of himself as an artist. When someone said he could not understand the music of one of these Rassumovsky quartets, Beethoven is supposed to have replied: 'Oh, they are not for you, but for a later age!' Seldom had artists before his time given much thought to posterity. The group of five quartets which Beethoven composed during the last years of his life constitute a large part of his output which scholars designate as belonging to his third, or late period, when his creative mind was still growing and moving in new directions. As with the late piano sonatas, these quartets include great sets of variations, and also fugues, a form which specially interested Beethoven as he grew older. The quartet movement published separately, because of its unique difficulties, is an immense fugue, known as the *Grosse Fuge* ('Great Fugue', opus 133). Today, however, this is often performed as Beethoven originally intended, as the last movement to the Quartet in B flat major (opus 130). Another famous piece of music from these late quartets is the slow movement to the Quartet in A minor (opus 132). Beethoven headed this: 'Holy song of thanksgiving to the Godhead, by one recovered from sickness', a moving testimony to the many illnesses, as well as almost total deafness, which he had to struggle against during the last years of his life.

Throughout his life, Beethoven wrote most of his music in the form of symphonies, concertos, sonatas, trios and string quartets. To this extent he continued the classical traditions of Haydn, Mozart and other musicians of the 18th century. On the other hand, he conveyed a great deal of personal expression through his music. From remarks he himself made, many of his compositions are associated in some way with his private life—even those without any particular title or nickname. The first movement of the piano sonata in E minor (opus 90) Beethoven described as 'a struggle between the head and the heart,' while the second movement he called 'a conversation with the beloved'. These descriptions probably allude to another of his patrons, Prince Lichnovsky, who had been divorced and after much heart-searching had recently married again. This side to Beethoven's music, and the obvious emotional intensity of much of it, belonged to the world of romantic art as it developed in the 19th century. Indeed, right through the 19th century almost every great composer— Schubert, Schumann, Mendelssohn, Berlioz, Liszt, Brahms, Wagner—found some special inspiration in the music of Beethoven.

Beethoven was a famous man in his own lifetime, but there were other contemporaries, or near contemporaries of his who were for a long time held in almost equally high regard. Reference to them today underlines the sad fact of how quickly fame and reputation can suffer in the affairs of men, for most of them are now quite neglected figures. Yet it is still interesting to hear their music, firstly because it often has real merit of its own, and secondly because the true greatness of an artist like Beethoven can be better understood

Napoleonic soldier playing the serpent, a cross between a brass and a woodwind instrument. Beethoven and Schubert both saw plenty of such soldiers in Vienna

by comparing his achievements with those who lived and worked at the same time.

Muzio Clementi (1752–1832) wrote much piano music which, like Beethoven's, acts as a bridge between the classical and romantic periods. Clementi's name was also once a household word as a piano manufacturer. Luigi Cherubini (1760–1842) was a most exalted figure during his own lifetime, whose operas, orchestral and chamber music were held in high esteem by Beethoven himself. Johann Hummel (1778–1837), a pupil of both Haydn and Mozart, was a celebrated pianist-composer. Ludwig Spohr (1784–1851), violinist, prolific composer and pioneer figure in the art of conducting, was as famous as Beethoven for much of the 19th century. Yet of all Beethoven's contemporaries, the composer who is now regarded as one of the greatest figures of the Viennese School was almost totally ignored both during his own brief lifetime and for years after his death. This was Franz Schubert (1797–1828).

The Viennese School, or Viennese Tradition, refers to the

succession of great composers who all lived and worked in Vienna, and who wrote much of their music in the form of symphonies, concertos, string quartets, sonatas, and other forms dating from the classical period. Mozart, Beethoven and, later, Brahms all moved to Vienna. Schubert was born there.

Schubert was the first of a long line of composers after Beethoven to complete nine symphonies, although the Eighth Symphony in B minor, known as the 'Unfinished', has only two movements instead of the usual four of the classical symphony. An attempt has been made to 'finish' this work, using material which it is believed Schubert might have had in mind for the purpose. The biggest of his symphonies is the Ninth Symphony in C major, known as 'The Great C major'. The manuscript of this work was completely forgotten about until years after its composer's death. Schubert also wrote many sonatas and other chamber works, including the string quartets in A minor (D804) and G major (D887), the String Quintet in C major (D956) and the Piano Sonata in B flat (D960). The 'D' stands for Otto Deutsch, a scholar who catalogued Schubert's works as Köchel had catalogued the works of Mozart.

The most memorable feature of many of these compositions is the melody. Schubert was perhaps the greatest melodist who has ever lived. His melodies seem to be the very essence of inspiration—tunes of an apparently effortless beauty. They unfold like the opening of a flower and, while some of the loveliest of them occur in Schubert's orchestral and instrumental music, they find their perfect expression in his songs, where they are complete in themselves.

Schubert's songs are often referred to by their equivalent German word of *Lieder*. This is because Schubert did much to establish a special tradition of song writing among German-speaking composers. Mozart composed some songs set to German words. Beethoven wrote a group of related songs, known as a song cycle, called *An die ferne Geliebte* ('To the Distant Beloved'). But it was Schubert who really established the *Lied*, or song, as a major new musical form. After him came a distinguished succession of *Lieder* composers, notably Schumann, Mendelssohn, Brahms and Hugo Wolf (1860–1903). Almost the whole of Wolf's output was in the form of songs.

Schubert himself wrote hundreds of songs. Some of them are seldom performed. Others, like *Heidenröslein* ('Wayside Rose'), *An die Musik* ('To Music') and *Ständchen* ('Serenade') are among the best loved pieces of music in the world. Schubert was so attracted to some of these songs that he used their melodies in other works. There is the Piano Quintet in A major (D667) known as *Die Forelle* ('The Trout') Quintet, because it uses the melody from the song of that name as the basis for a set of variations. For the same reason there is the String Quartet in D minor known as *Der Todt und das Mädchen* ('Death and the Maiden').

Schubert's greatest achievements in this field are the two big song cycles he wrote towards the end of his tragically short life. These have the collective titles of *Die schöne Müllerin* ('The Fair Maid of the Mill') and *Die Winterreise* ('The Winter Journey'). Each contains some of Schubert's finest melodies, and also examples of his genius for setting the scene or mood of a song by means of the piano accompaniment. The piano accompaniment is a vital ingredient in nearly all *Lieder*, and some pianists specialise in this branch of music.

Die schöne Müllerin and *Die Winterreise* both deal with the theme of unrequited love, and express a wide range of emotions, from joy and happiness to sorrow and despair. They also relate these emotions to the natural world of woods and streams, summer sun and winter snow. Such features are typical of much romantic art. The word 'romantic' in this context is not limited to the subject of love, or to a world of glamorous make-believe. The romantic movement of the 19th century was a whole way of thinking and feeling about the world, and how such thoughts and feelings could be expressed through philosophy and the arts.

The beginnings of the romantic movement date back to the ideas of some 18th century thinkers and writers, like the Swiss-French philosopher Jean Jacques Rousseau, who believed that each person has a right to develop his personality and talents in his own way. During the 18th century itself there was a movement called in German *Stürm und Drang* ('Storm and Stress'), because German artists had most to do with it. This movement conveyed a restless desire for more dramatic means of expression. It was largely confined to literature, although some 18th century composers, including C. P. E. Bach and Haydn, cultivated a correspondingly stormy or restless style in some of their music. However, the real start of the romantic movement was early in the 19th century, following upon the social upheavals of the French Revolution. Artists like Beethoven and the Spanish painter Francisco Goya began to claim a special position in society by expressing feelings and ideas that mattered to them personally. Many romantic artists also felt the need to escape from what they saw as the artificiality or false values of society, and, like the English poet William Wordsworth, seek truth and beauty through a love of nature. Above all, they aimed at a greater degree of self-expression, creating for themselves new forms and styles if existing ones did not suit their needs.

The piano was a favourite instrument with romantic composers, and they often used it to convey the idea of improvisation—of having sat down at the instrument and allowed the inspiration of the moment to guide their fingers over the keys. The art of improvisation was centuries old. At first, indeed, all music was improvised, since in the earliest times, before any proper instruments existed and thousands of years before music was written down, that was the only way it could come into being. By the 18th century improvisation, within the forms of the time, was widely practised, and J. S. Bach was a great master of the art at the organ and other keyboard instruments.

The idea of such free-flowing expression had a special appeal for romantic musicians. Beethoven was renowned as a young man for his ability to improvise at the piano, and the first movement of his so-called 'Moonlight' Sonata, with its dreamy, reflective mood, clearly looks forward to the great age of romantic piano music. So do some of the short piano pieces he wrote called Bagatelles.

Schubert wrote one group of short piano pieces called Impromptus, and another group entitled *Moments Musicaux* ('Musical Moments'). These different titles all suggest music of an improvisatory character.

Robert Schumann (1810–1856) wrote most of his piano music in the form of groups of related short pieces which brilliantly convey the idea of spontaneous inspiration and self-discovery. The way they contain allusions to the composer's private life, thoughts and moods also make them typical of much romantic music. Schumann was particularly fond of taking the names of people or places associated with his life and applying the letters of such names to the corresponding musical notes as the basis for a composition. The *Abegg Variations* owe their existence to a friend of the composer whose name was Meta Abegg. The set of pieces called *Carnaval* are based on the letters of musical notes which also spell the name of a town associated with Schumann's love life. The *Davidsbündler-Tänze* ('Dances of the League of David') refer to a group of progressive young musicians, including Schumann, dedicated to fighting the 'philistines' or musical conservatives of their day. These dances also express the two contrasted sides to Schumann's character; the dreamy, poetic side, which he called 'Eusebius', and the fiery, passionate side, which he called 'Florestan', after characters familiar to him from German literature. Schumann, almost as interested in literature as music, was also critic, propagandist and founder of a famous musical journal. As a composer he also wrote some of the finest *Lieder*—many of them inspired by his marriage to Clara Wieck, pianist and composer in her own right—four symphonies and the Piano Concerto in A minor. This concerto was a model for later composers, especially Grieg.

Another master of romantic piano music was Frédéric Chopin (1810–1849). He wrote two piano concertos for himself to play at concerts, and three piano sonatas, though these are different in character and in construction from the classical-style sonatas of Haydn, Mozart and Beethoven. One of them, the Sonata in B flat minor, contains the famous Funeral March. Otherwise, almost the whole of Chopin's output consists of short piano pieces. The orchestral score of the well-known ballet *Les Sylphides* was compiled from these pieces years after the composer's death.

Chopin lived in Paris for most of his life, but his mother was Polish and he was born in that country. Poland had suffered from centuries of foreign invasion and persecution, and Chopin, moved by a deep sense of injustice, used themes and rhythms from Polish folk music to express his own devotion to the land of his birth and to the cause of Polish freedom. His most numerous group of pieces are his mazurkas, based on a Polish peasant dance; while his most openly patriotic pieces are his *polonaises*—the French name for a type of Polish national dance—as thrilling today as when they were composed.

Chopin's other major groups of piano works are the nocturnes (a poetic and dreamy type of composition whose style he inherited from the Irish composer John Field), waltzes, ballades, preludes and studies. These twenty-four studies (or *études*, to give them their French title) belong to that category of composition whose source of inspiration is some point of technique. Each is intended as a technical exercise, but each is also a superb example of some aspect of Chopin's piano style. Some of Chopin's compositions have been given romantic-sounding nicknames. There is the so-called 'Revolutionary' Study (opus 10 no. 12 in C minor), the 'Winter Wind' Study (opus 25 no. 11 in A minor), and the 'Raindrop' Prelude (opus 28 no. 15 in D flat major). But Chopin did not give such names to any of his works, and their true poetic meaning lies entirely in the music.

Although Chopin's music often sounds as though it were improvised, he was a very fastidious composer and concerned that every note of music he wrote down was exactly right. Some of his music is difficult to play, but it is always perfectly suited to the physical nature and character of the piano. Such high standards of craftsmanship were not always upheld by Franz Liszt (1811–1886), the most astonishing pianist-composer of the romantic period.

During Liszt's long and eventful career the piano emerged as an instrument of really strong construction and great technical refinement, capable of producing thunderous cascades of notes or the softest gradations of sound. It acted as a challenge to many 19th century musicians, who wrote for it and played upon it music demanding phenomenal skill and effort. The word which describes such music and its performance is virtuosity. The Austrian Sigismund Thalberg (1812–1871) and the Frenchman Charles

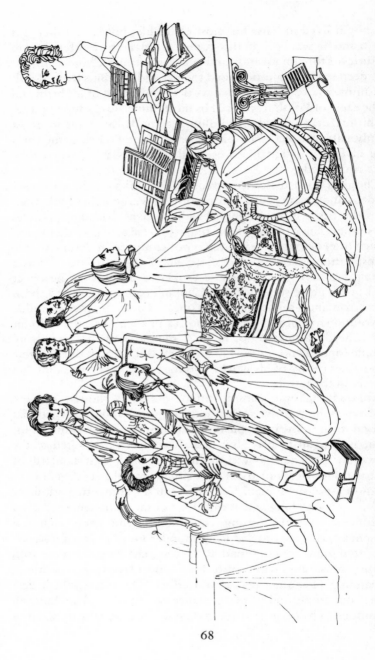

Liszt at the piano surrounded by adoring friends, including Paganini and Rossini who stand directly behind him. A large bust of Beethoven stands on the piano

Morhange (1833–1888), who adopted the name Alkan, played or wrote music which made extreme demands upon both the performer and the instrument. But no piano virtuoso could rival Liszt, for showmanship was a part of such music, and Liszt was not only a dazzling performer, but also strikingly handsome. The practice of playing sideways-on to the audience probably started with him. By this method, with the lid raised, the sound could more effectively be directed at the audience, although detractors said it was because Liszt wanted to display his beautiful profile! One contemporary print shows young women fainting in his presence, just as though he were a pop star. A cartoon of the time shows a piano collapsing under his breathtaking assault.

Theatrical display and what are called piano pyrotechnics (fireworks) lie behind such compositions as the Hungarian Rhapsodies, and Liszt's many transcriptions for the piano of popular themes from operas. The only other musician to create as great a sensation was the Italian violinist Nicolo Paganini (1782–1840). People said he was in league with the Devil, because of his strange, deformed appearance as well as because of the extraordinary tricks of virtuosity he could perform on his chosen instrument. In fact, his incredible virtuosity was due, in part at least, to the merciless training he received from his father, who made him practise as a child to the point of collapse. Paganini wrote a group of violin pieces called *capriccios* (an Italian word describing a fairly lively, light-hearted composition), and one of these is famous today because first Brahms and then Rachmaninov used it as the basis for works of their own. However, Paganini is not considered an important composer, whereas there was a much more serious side to Liszt's music.

In his Piano Sonata in B minor, Liszt pioneered the idea of welding together the structure of the sonata into a single-movement form. Then, as he grew older, Liszt became very advanced in his thinking about the use of harmony. And he played a big part in the development of *programme music*, or 'illustrative music' as it is sometimes called.

Programme music is intended to depict a particular scene or mood, or to describe in some way the events of a story. It is the opposite of *absolute music*, which is supposed to contain nothing but purely musical ideas. Vivaldi, Couperin and others before them had often written music which contained some kind of descriptive 'programme'. Haydn wrote a very striking piece of orchestral music to depict the idea of chaos as the opening to his oratorio *The Creation*. But it was composers of the romantic period who really concentrated on writing such music. Most of Liszt's compositions are based on some kind of 'programme'. One of his largest choral and orchestral works is the *Faust* Symphony, inspired by the legend of Dr Faustus, the scholar and mystic who sold his soul to the Devil, or Mephistopheles, for knowledge and power. This was a theme which fascinated many romantic composers because it formed the greatest work of Germany's greatest poet, Wolfgang von Goethe. In other orchestral works, Liszt did as he had done with the piano sonata, and condensed his ideas into a single, extended movement. By combining this arrangement with a clearly defined 'programme', he produced a new kind of orchestral composition which he called a 'symphonic poem'. In this way he helped to shape the course of orchestral music during the romantic period.

The growth and development of orchestral music in the 19th century is one of the most remarkable chapters in the history of music. At the beginning of the century, most composers were still writing for an orchestra of about thirty-five players, as required by Haydn and others of the classical period. Composers like Beethoven began to enlarge upon this complement of players in their compositions, and by the end of the century composers were often writing for an orchestra of over a hundred musicians. Each of the basic 'families' of instruments had grown numerically, and there were many instruments added as well which had not previously been part of the orchestra, ranging from the harp to a whole group of percussion instruments like the xylophone, tubular bells, triangle, cymbals and gong. Some instruments, notably in the brass section, were also improved technically so that much more interesting and imaginative music could be written for them.

All this encouraged much new thinking on the subject of orchestration—the art or technique of writing music for the orchestra. Before the 19th century composers had, as a rule, written in the orchestral style of their time. During and after the 19th century, many composers created individual styles of orchestration that were almost like trademarks of their work.

One of the first outstanding orchestrators was the Frenchman Hector Berlioz (1803–1869). Berlioz, like Liszt, helped to create the popular image of the romantic artist by the example of his own life and work. At the time when he settled in Paris, that city was already a world centre of romantic art, literature and music. Also working there was the artist Eugène Delacroix, the writers and dramatists Honoré de Balzac, Victor Hugo, Alexandre Dumas and Georges Sands (pen name of the woman novelist whose numerous scandals included her affair with Chopin), Chopin himself and Liszt. There was also much political agitation following the final downfall of Napoleon and the brief restoration of the monarchy. It was a colourful time and place in which to live. It produced the popular idea of the Bohemian artist, free from the usual restraints of society and free also to half starve himself in a garret. Puccini's opera *La Bohème* is set in Paris at this time. Berlioz had abandoned his medical studies against his father's will, and himself went hungry as a music student. Still as a young man he fell desperately in love with an Irish actress named Harriet Smithson, whom he later married. This inspired him to write the *Symphonie Fantastique* ('Fantastic Symphony') which is about the delirium of a young man, crossed in love, and contains such images as a March to the Scaffold and a Witches' Sabbath. For other compositions Berlioz called for an orchestra and chorus of hundreds. 'Mad Hector of the Flaming Locks' he was called, and as Liszt was caricatured as a pianist, so Berlioz was depicted wildly directing a colossal orchestra which included cannons!

But like Liszt, Berlioz was also a very serious artist. He wrote a book about orchestration in which he discussed and analysed the qualities of all the instruments of the orchestra and how they could be used in different combinations, very much as a painter might discuss the blending of different coloured paints. The *Symphonie Fantastique*, the symphony called *Harold en Italie* ('Harold in Italy'), and the two concert overtures (that is, overtures written specially for the concert hall) *Le Carnaval Romain* ('Roman Carnival') and *Le Corsair* (a North African pirate) are all brilliant examples of his own orchestral style. At the same time, Berlioz could compose very quiet and gentle music, as in his oratorio *L'Enfance du Christ* ('The Childhood of Christ').

Berlioz, like many romantic composers, was often inspired by works of literature. He, too, wrote a work based on the Faust legend, the dramatic oratorio *La Damnation de Faust*. Shakespeare was another source of inspiration to him, and he composed what he called a 'dramatic symphony', including parts for a solo voice and chorus, based on the play *Romeo and Juliet*.

Another of Shakespeare's plays, *A Midsummer Night's Dream*, inspired Felix Mendelssohn–Bartholdy (1809–1847) to write some of his finest orchestral music. This music is called *incidental music*, meaning that it was originally intended to introduce, or very occasionally accompany certain parts of the play. Mendelssohn, as he is nearly always called, composed his overture to *A Midsummer Night's Dream* when he was only seventeen, but no one has written orchestral music of greater delicacy or filled with a finer sense of magic and wonder. Another of his descriptive works for the orchestra is the *Hebrides* overture, or 'Fingal's Cave', inspired by a tour of the Western Isles of Scotland. The scenery of the Scottish Highlands, and the many romantic legends attached to Scottish history, made a strong appeal to 19th century composers and writers.

Mendelssohn was an all-round musician and a conductor of distinction. The art or technique of conducting developed side by side with the increasing size of orchestras and the increasing complexity of orchestral music. Before the 19th century, musicians did sometimes beat time for an orchestra or choir. In France there had been a tradition of beating time on the floor with a heavy staff—Lully died from blood poisoning after accidentally banging his foot in this way. But for a long time, the leading violin player, still known as the leader in British orchestras (and as concert master in Germany and the United States), was the virtual director of a performance. Another kind of orchestral direction was frequently provided by a *continuo* player—someone who accompanied the performance on a keyboard instrument. Continuo playing was also used to guide singers through recitative passages in operas and oratorios. None of these practices, however, was adequate for the performance of most 19th century orchestral music. What was needed was a proper conductor; someone to study the score, lead the orchestra through detailed rehearsals and direct the performance from a central position where he could be seen by all members of the orchestra and so exercise a proper control over the performance.

Compositions like the symphonies of Beethoven or the programme music works of Liszt and Berlioz had so many aspects to them, relating to matters of tempo and dynamics and instrumentation, that they were also open to a good deal of individual interpretation by conductors. Succeeding generations of conductors, including such celebrated figures as Wilhelm Furtwängler and Arturo Toscanini, directed performances of orchestral works and operas which, because they are preserved on record, have come to be considered almost as significant as the music itself. Pianists and other instrumental soloists, such as Artur Schnabel, Walter Gieseking, Alfred Cortot, Pablo Casals and Fritz Kreisler, are similarly revered as great interpretative artists.

Orchestras themselves began to be organised in new ways in the 19th century. Many of the old aristocratic families of the 18th century were impoverished or dispersed as a result of the Napoleonic Wars, and their system of aristocratic patronage was brought to an end. In their place came bankers, tradesmen, factory owners and other relatively well-off people who lived in the rapidly expanding towns and cities of the Industrial Revolution, and who paid to go to concerts. Orchestras were formed on this new kind of commercial basis. One of the first to be established in this way was the Leipzig Gewandhaus Orchestra, the Gewandhaus being a trading hall in the city where concerts were given from the end of the 18th century. Mendelssohn became the conductor of this famous orchestra, and by working regularly with such a group of musicians was able to raise the standards of orchestral discipline and performance.

In his capacity as a conductor Mendelssohn also did much to

revive interest in the music of J. S. Bach. He gave the first performance of the *St Matthew Passion* since Bach's death. Mendelssohn's deep respect for the past influenced much of his own music. His Violin Concerto in E minor, written in one continuous movement, is one of the best-loved of all romantic concertos, but most of his symphonies and chamber works adhere quite strictly to sonata form and other features of the classical period. Even his groups of small piano pieces which he called *Lieder ohne Worte* ('Songs Without Words'), though they have romantic charm, are carefully fashioned and restrained. The two best-known of these pieces are the 'Spring Song' and 'Bees' Wedding', though these were not Mendelssohn's titles.

Johannes Brahms (1833–1897) was equally attached to the musical past, and did not carry romantic music forward in any striking new directions. His critics judged him to be a somewhat reactionary figure, while his admirers praised him as a stabilising influence in what they regarded as a wild and uncertain artistic world. Brahms himself was not a romantic personality in the image of Berlioz or Liszt. He was a serious-minded north German from Hamburg, big and handsome as a young man, but increasingly solitary and gruff as he grew older. Schumann was one of the first to recognise his gifts, calling Brahms his 'young eagle' and writing enthusiastically about him in his capacity as a music critic. After the former's tragic mental breakdown and death, his widow, Clara Schumann, remained one of Brahms' few real friends and companions. She was often the first to hear from him of a new composition, and he frequently sought her musical opinion and advice. But, like Beethoven, he did not marry, and again like his great predecessor, settled in Vienna and devoted himself to composition.

It was the example of Beethoven's life and work which for a long time weighed so heavily upon Brahms. He spent over twenty years shaping and re-shaping his First Symphony in C minor, believing that his work would have to stand comparison with that of Beethoven. His remaining symphonies (no. 2 in D major, no. 3 in F major, and no. 4 in E minor) were composed with far less heart-searching and effort. They are works of Brahms' full maturity, composed in the symphonic tradition of Haydn, Mozart and Beethoven, with ideas growing out of each other and with a strong sense of musical logic and attention to form. In his Fourth Symphony Brahms looked back even further in time, by concluding the work with a movement in the form of a passacaglia, a special type of variation form which J. S. Bach and other composers of the baroque period had often used.

Brahms wrote other major works for the concert hall, including the Variations on the St Anthony Chorale (formerly known as 'Variations on a Theme of Haydn'), two piano concertos, a violin concerto, and a 'double concerto' for violin and cello. His greatest choral work, *Ein deutsches Requiem* ('A German Requiem'), is not a setting of the Catholic Mass, but sets to music passages from Luther's German translation of the Bible.

Brahms enriched the traditions of his predecessors in many other ways. He followed in the path of Schubert and Schumann by writing a large number of *Lieder*; and he composed a large and impressive body of instrumental and chamber music. This body of music includes sonatas for the piano, the violin and the cello, string quartets, and other compositions for familiar instrumental combinations. But Brahms wrote other chamber works for more unusual instrumental groupings, such as the Trio in E flat for piano, violin and horn. It is characteristic of Brahms, with his strong sense of tradition, that he wrote this work specifically for the natural horn—an instrument modelled closely on the old hunting horn, with one long coiled tube—although horns with valves, giving them a wider range of notes and greater flexibility, had been introduced earlier in the century. However, there was a romantic side to Brahms, so that these works, like the symphonies and concertos, sometimes sound very lyrical and mellow, sometimes very dramatic, and are full of subtle changes of harmony and tonal 'colour'. Brahms even went so far as to write some groups of piano pieces with such openly romantic titles as 'rhapsody' and 'intermezzo'. He also wrote a set of sixteen waltzes and some light-hearted Hungarian Dances which reveal his love of the waltz music of the Strauss family of Vienna and the kind of gaiety it symbolised.

One of the origins of the waltz was a simple type of Austrian peasant dance called the *Ländler*, which had three beats to the bar played at a slow, sedate pace. The three beats to the bar of the waltz were played at about twice the speed, producing the characteristic

Conducting styles: Brahms (left) and Wagner

lilt and making it the most popular dance rhythm of all time. The first great composer of waltzes was Johann Strauss (1804–1849), but it was his son, also christened Johann, who wrote the best-loved waltzes of all, including *The Blue Danube* and *Tales from the Vienna Woods*. Johann Strauss the Younger (1825–1899) also wrote many polkas—a lively kind of dance from Bohemia—and for the stage he composed operettas. The word 'operetta' means a little opera, but more especially it describes a light entertainment with a romantic, sometimes comic, plot, and tuneful music. Johann Strauss' most celebrated operetta is *Die Fledermaus* ('The Bat'), the bat in question being one of the character's fancy dress costume.

Jacques Offenbach (1819–1880), who was born in Germany, wrote equally successful operettas, or comic operas, for the Paris stage. During the 19th century Paris and Vienna shared the reputation as the world's two most pleasure-loving cities. And while Vienna had the Strauss family and the waltz, Offenbach gave Paris the can-can, in the sense that he included the most famous of all can-can dances in his operetta *Orpheus in the Underworld*. His opera *The Tales of Hoffmann*, based on stories by the German writer E. T. A. Hoffmann, is a more serious and substantial work.

It is also one of several famous musical works which had to be completed after its composer's death. Mozart's Requiem and Puccini's opera *Turandot* are two others.

Opera meant something totally different to Richard Wagner (1813–1883). He lived through the main period of the Industrial Revolution, when factories and railways transformed the landscape of large parts of Europe and America and towns and cities took on the character and appearance that they have largely retained to this day. The men responsible for all this, whether they were engineers like Isambard Kingdom Brunel or industrialists like Andrew Carnegie, regarded hard work as the highest virtue, and sheer size and scale as the finest rewards of their labour and enterprise. Writers of the period, like Charles Dickens, Honoré de Balzac and Leo Tolstoy were no less industrious, producing a succession of long and weighty novels. But for hard, unremitting work, and for the scale and scope of his ideas, no one could compare with Richard Wagner.

Wagner's mind brimmed over with ideas about philosophy and politics and the art of the future, which he wrote about in numerous books and essays. And from many of these ideas emerged the longest, most complex and visionary operas that anyone is ever likely to produce. To achieve all this, Wagner did not lock himself away in a room for years on end. It was a part of his nature to need fine clothes, be surrounded by beautiful objects, even to have the very air about him filled with rare and exotic perfumes. 'I must have beauty and brilliance and light,' he declared. 'The world owes this to me.' So he spent a great deal of time and energy borrowing or cajoling money out of people, in order to live in the style of luxury he considered necessary for him to fulfil his stupendous plans. He was also a passionate man where women were concerned, and became involved in some of the most notorious scandals of the age. And at one stage, his participation in revolutionary politics ended in pursuit by the police and banishment from his native state of Saxony.

As a composer, Wagner's aim from the very start of his career was to further the cause of German opera and put it on an equal footing with the far older operatic traditions of Italy and France. Mozart and Beethoven, in their different ways, had begun to establish a tradition of German opera with works like *Die Zauberflöte* and *Fidelio*.Beethoven's contemporary, Carl Maria von Weber (1786–1826), was another important figure in this development. His most famous opera is *Der Freischütz* ('The Marksman'). The plot concerns a young man who enters into a pact with the Devil in order to win a shooting contest. There is a scene where the hero, Max, meets the Devil in a grim and frightening place called the Wolf's Glen. Weber's very atmospheric music for this scene is a high point in early German romantic opera.

Wagner's early works were a continuation of this kind of German romantic opera. They include *Der fliegende Holländer* ('The Flying Dutchman'), inspired by the legend of a Dutch sea captain cursed to sail the oceans forever unless redeemed by the love of a woman; *Tannhäuser*, the story of a medieval German minstrel torn between sexual and spiritual love; and *Lohengrin*, based on one of the legends about the Holy Grail, the cup which Christ was supposed to have used at the Last Supper. These operas are still fairly conventional in the way they are constructed, but they already contain music more powerful and dramatic than any yet heard in an opera house. The prelude to *Lohengrin*, depicting the gradual descent from heaven of the Holy Grail in a blaze of glory, is a particularly famous piece of music.

After *Lohengrin*, however, the ideas which Wagner had been thinking about for years, concerning the future of opera and of art in general, began to take definite shape in his mind. Other composers before him, notably Gluck, had sometimes considered the need to reform opera in one way or another; to rid it of many of its conventions and make people take it more seriously as an art form. But Wagner's ideas went far beyond this. He wanted to create a new, super art form, or *Gesammtkunstwerk* as he called it, meaning 'union of the arts'. From the standpoint of the symphony, Beethoven had already been working towards the same kind of idea of a universal art in works like the 'Choral' Symphony—a composition which was a great source of inspiration to Wagner himself.

The principal work in which Wagner put his own ideas into practice was the gigantic *Der Ring des Nibelungen* ('The Ring of the Nibelung'), comprising over seventeen hours of music. 'The Ring' is in four parts: *Das Rheingold* ('The Rhinegold'), intended as a prologue to the whole cycle; *Die Walküre* ('The Valkyries'); *Siegfried*; and *Götterdämmerung* ('Twilight of the Gods'). Some people liken this scheme to a huge operatic symphony, with the four individual operas corresponding to the traditional four movements of the symphony. It is based upon old Norse and Teutonic legends about a time when the world was peopled by

Brunnhilde rides into the flames of Siegfried's funeral pyre in the closing scene of *Götterdämmerung*

gods, giants and a race of dwarfs, the Nibelungs. Wagner spent years pouring over these old legends, gradually reshaping them in his mind into a saga about a rock of gold stolen from the river Rhine. This gold is fashioned into a magic ring, but one which carries a terrible curse and brings tragedy to all who seek or possess it. Only when the ring is finally restored to the Rhine, whose waters rise up to flood the earth, is the world made pure again.

Most operatic composers leave somebody else to write their libretto for them, but Wagner was never the kind of man who could have entered into such a collaboration. Everything about his work he had to do for himself. So he first planned and wrote out the libretto of 'The Ring', using a style of archaic German which he considered suitable for the character of the story. He also included the most detailed stage directions. For the opening scene of *Das Rheingold* he instructed: 'Greenish twilight, lighter above, darker below. The upper part of the scene is filled with moving water, which restlessly streams from right to left. Towards the bottom the waters resolve themselves into a fine mist, so that the space to a man's height from the stage seems free from the water which floats like a train of clouds over the gloomy depths.' These were very exacting requirements at a time when theatres and opera houses had virtually none of the electrical and other technical aids which producers can use today.

When Wagner did start work on the score, the music was very different from any that had been written before. No longer were the singers given passages of recitative or spoken dialogue, followed by set arias. Instead they declaimed their lines, sometimes in short passages, sometimes in long, unbroken lines of melody, in which each note and phrase was intended to underline the meaning and psychological significance of the words.

Equally new was Wagner's use of a device called a *Leitmotiv* ('leading motive'). This might be a short theme or pattern of notes, or even just a chord, intended to represent a particular character, object, idea or mood. Other romantic composers, taking their cue from such works as Beethoven's Fifth Symphony, had sometimes used a recurring motto theme to give a composition a special sense of unity and identity. Berlioz's name for such a musical device was *idée fixe* ('fixed idea'). But Wagner's use of the *Leitmotiv* played a much more fundamental part in his radical new musical thinking.

In 'The Ring' there are hundreds of *Leitmotiven*, to represent all the characters, objects, concepts and emotions embodied in the drama. Sometimes Wagner created two or more *Leitmotiven* for the same character or idea, introducing one or other of them into the score depending upon the precise circumstances of the action at that point. The effect on the music is to build up an increasingly rich tapestry of sound, as each *Leitmotiv* is introduced and then woven into the score.

The orchestra itself was of immense importance in this process. Wagner enlarged it so that at moments of climax it was capable of delivering an overwhelming body of sound. He exploited all the latest technical improvements to instruments, often writing passages for orchestral players which previously only virtuoso soloists might have been expected to perform. And he added some new instruments of his own design, like the so-called Wagner tuba, though this more closely ressembled a horn.

Wagner worked on 'The Ring' until even his energies and faith in what he was doing began to flag. The work had so absorbed him that he had earned no money from any other source, and had not heard a note of his own music actually played for years. He also saw no prospect of anything as costly and revolutionary as 'The Ring' ever being staged. To his friend Liszt he wrote, 'I have led my young Siegfried into the lovely solitudes of the forest. There I have left him under a linden tree, and, with tears from the depths of my heart, said farewell to him.'

But so powerful were Wagner's creative impulses that he almost immediately started work on two of his other greatest operas, or 'music dramas' as he called them. *Tristan und Isolde* is based on old Celtic legends from Cornwall and Brittany. It is a story about a love potion and its effect upon the two characters, Tristan and Isolde, who take it, and of the tragic events that follow. The opera contains some of the most passionate and obsessive love music ever written, at least partly inspired by Wagner's affair with a young married woman named Mathilde Wesendonck, whose husband had given the composer financial support.

The music of *Tristan und Isolde* is also of great interest and significance from a technical point of view. It represents another major aspect of Wagner's style, called 'chromaticism'. Going back hundreds of years into the history of Western, or European music, composers had written their individual pieces of music in a particular mode or, since the Renaissance, in a particular key, either of which provided the music with a firm harmonic foundation. Composers became more and more imaginative and adventurous in the way they might move, or modulate, from one key to another during the course of the music, but they always made sure that they finally returned to their 'home' key. Wagner's 'chromaticism' consisted of constant and rapid modulations of the music from one key to another, which might be compared to constantly shifting patterns or shades of colour. He developed this technique to such a degree that from the very opening chords of the prelude to *Tristan und Isolde* the music seems to float free of any particular key or tonal foundation. The music to this prelude, and Wagner's 'chromaticism' in general, had a very important influence on the future course of musical thought and practice.

Die Meistersinger von Nürnberg is set in Nuremberg during the 16th century, when it was one of the most illustrious cities in Germany, noted for its many fine churches and other buildings and for the pageantry of its famous trades guilds. The opera is called a comedy, but it is by no means a comedy in the older Italian sense of *opera buffa*. The only comic character is the town clerk, Sextus Beckmesser, who ends up making a fool of himself at the annual song contest organised by the city's college of musicians, the Mastersingers themselves. This character is a thinly disguised caricature of a real person, Eduard Hanslick, an influential Viennese music critic of Wagner's time and an opponent of his music. Beckmesser was Wagner's way of getting his own back. Otherwise, *Die Meistersinger* is far more an expression of love, friendship and happiness, and the music is warm, golden and optimistic throughout. It is also beautifully constructed as a piece of writing for the theatre. The prelude to the whole opera, a real curtain-raiser, introduces many of the themes and weaves them together in a way that both creates an atmosphere of excitement and expectancy and suggests the polyphonic styles of renaissance music.

The optimism which Wagner conveyed in *Die Meistersinger* turned out to be justified in relation to his own career. For just when things looked blackest for him, he suddenly received generous support from Ludwig II of Bavaria. This monarch had read Wagner's books, heard some of his earlier music and became obsessed with the composer's work and ideas. He was a strange, morbid young man who spent vast sums of public money building fairy-tale castles in the Alps, and was later declared insane and deposed. But he gave Wagner the chances he needed to realise his greatest ambitions. He completed his work on 'The Ring', and designed and supervised the construction at Bayreuth in Bavaria of an opera house specially intended for the performance of his works.

Wagner's festival theatre at Bayreuth

Wagner's last 'music drama' was *Parsifal*, another work based on the theme of the Holy Grail. He regarded this as a semi-religious work, to be performed only at Bayreuth. After Wagner's death his widow, Cosima, Liszt's daughter with whom he had eloped some years before, tried to honour her husband's wishes in this respect. But *Parsifal*, together with all Wagner's other operas and 'music dramas', was soon being produced in opera houses all over the world.

Wagner had to fight hard for many years to get his operas performed, but once he had secured a reputation his music swept through Europe and America like a tidal wave. It overwhelmed not only audiences but many other composers who either copied Wagner's techniques or were inspired by his ideas. They are sometimes called post-Wagnerians.

Anton Bruckner (1824–1896) in Austria wrote nine symphonies that generally proceed with the same broad, measured pace of Wagner, and often sound very like Wagner's own orchestration. The long, flowing themes and passages of rising orchestral sound remind some listeners of a magnificent landscape of towering mountain peaks, very like the Alpine landscape of the composer's own country. Bruckner was a devout Catholic, and for other listeners his symphonies suggest a great cathedral or the rich, glowing colours of stained glass. He also wrote several specifically religious works, similar in style, including a *Te Deum*, a special Latin hymn in praise of God. An interesting oddity is an early version of a Bruckner symphony which is now known as Symphony no. 0.

Gustav Mahler (1860–1911), also Austrian, was one of the most celebrated conductors of his time, especially in the field of opera, and held important operatic posts in Budapest, Hamburg, Vienna and New York. Mahler did not write any operas himself, but as Wagner regarded opera as an art form capable of expressing a whole world of thought and feeling, so Mahler regarded the symphony, completing nine of the most complex and ambitious symphonies ever written. However, he was very interested in writing music for the voice, and four of these symphonies include important parts either for solo voices, or for soloists plus a chorus. His Eighth Symphony is known as the 'Symphony of a Thousand' because it requires soloists and a chorus of several hundreds as well as a very large orchestra. In addition, Mahler wrote several large-scale song cycles for solo voices and orchestra, including *Kindertotenlieder* ('Songs on the Death of Children') and *Das Lied von der Erde* ('The Song of the Earth'), this being a group of settings of old Chinese poems. From a purely musical point of view, Mahler's symphonies and song cycles are significant because of their original orchestration and harmonies and the way they anticipate many 20th century developments.

The German composer Richard Strauss (1864–1949)—no relation to the Strauss family of Vienna—developed further Wagner's orchestral techniques. He was still only in his early twenties when he wrote a symphonic poem called *Don Juan* (the same character as Mozart's Don Giovanni), but the brilliance of his orchestration astonished the musical world. In other symphonic poems, like *Till Eulenspiegel*, inspired by a legendary German folk hero, and *Ein Heldenleben* ('A Hero's Life'), Strauss wrote orchestral music of increasing length and complexity. This latter work is a piece of autobiography in music, the 'hero' being the composer himself.

In some of his other symphonic poems Strauss got as close as any composer to portraying particular scenes or events in music. *Don Quixote*, sub-titled 'Fantastic Variations on a Theme of Knightly Character', is based on episodes from the classic novel by Miguel Cervantes. It has important parts for a solo cello and solo viola, representing Don Quixote himself and his squire Sancho Panza. There is one passage for brass instruments realistically recalling the bleating of sheep, and another which describes the Don's imaginary ride on a flying horse. For this passage Strauss made use of a wind machine, a device which creates the sound of rushing wind when a large drum is revolved inside a tightly stretched piece of canvas. This was one of several special-effects instruments which had been added to the huge post-Wagnerian orchestra.

Strauss also wrote operas which are a continuation of the tradition of German opera from Weber to Wagner. *Salome*, based on a play by Oscar Wilde, and *Elektra*, based on the classic play by the Greek dramatist Sophocles, contain music which shocked early audiences because of the violent or lurid scenes that went with it. Today Strauss's best-loved opera is *Der Rosenkavalier* ('The Cavalier of the Rose'), one of several he wrote in collaboration with the poet and dramatist Hugo von Hofmannsthal as his librettist. It is set in 18th-century Vienna, and Strauss was able to evoke a very romantic and nostalgic atmosphere with some of his richest and sweetest-sounding music. The score includes a set of waltzes—the composer's tribute to his Viennese namesakes.

Max Reger (1873–1916) was in many ways quite a different sort of man to the other German and Austrian post-Wagnerian composers. Like Brahms and Mendelssohn, he had a great liking and respect for the music of pre-romantic times. He composed numerous fugues, passacaglias and other pieces normally associated with the time of J. S. Bach, and the organ was his favourite instrument. However, just as much a part of Reger's style was his chromatic harmony—the rapid shifting from one key to another—which was such a strong feature of Wagner's own musical style. The *Variations on a Theme of Mozart* for orchestra are a good example of this side to Reger's music.

Despite Wagner's own immense achievements and influence, he was not the only important operatic composer of his time. In Italy there was Giuseppe Verdi (1813–1901), who inherited a tradition of opera going back to Monteverdi and the very beginnings of opera itself.

An especially rich period in Italian opera had preceded Verdi early in the 19th century. Gaetano Donizetti (1797–1848) and Vincenzo Bellini (1801–1835) were masters of a style of operatic writing called *bel canto* ('beautiful singing') which required the singers, especially sopranos, to display great vocal agility as well as a beautiful tone of voice. Donizetti and Bellini wrote, with equal success, both tragic and comic operas, one of the most popular of these being Donizetti's comic opera *Don Pasquale*.

Gioacchino Rossini (1792–1868) was the third important Italian operatic composer to precede Verdi earlier in the 19th century, and to write in the *bel canto* style. Rossini was superb at creating a sense of excitement by taking an attractive little theme and repeating it over and over again, all the time emphasizing the rhythm and increasing the volume of orchestral sound. This technique earned him the nickname of 'Signor Crescendo', and in his own time he was regarded as a very noisy composer. But no one else has written music of quite such vitality. *Il barbiere di Siviglia* ('The Barber of

Seville')—which contains many of the same characters as Mozart's *Le Nozze di Figaro*—is the only Rossini opera to be regularly performed today, but the overtures to many of his other operas, notably *La scala di seta* ('The Silken Ladder'), *La gazza ladra* ('The Thieving Magpie') and, above all, *Guillaume Tell*, are among the most popular works in the concert hall. *Guillaume Tell*, based on Johann Schiller's dramatic account of the famous Swiss hero William Tell, was given this French version of the title because Rossini composed it for the Paris Opera. As well as being about a national hero, it was the kind of opera described as 'heroic', and was planned on an appropriately large scale. It was also Rossini's last opera. He had worked hard, made a fortune, and at the age of 37 until his death nearly forty years later, settled in Paris to lead a life of ease. Only occasionally did he write any more music, and never anything as demanding as an opera.

Verdi, like Rossini and other Italian operatic composers before him, wrote to please the Italian public, who liked singable melodies and a libretto that allowed for plenty of stage action. Consequently, Verdi's operas move at a comparatively fast pace. At the same time, the voice nearly always takes pride of place. Verdi's operas are also very varied in terms of style and plot, for he was not concerned with the kind of philosophical or musical theories that occupied so much of Wagner's time.

As a young man, Verdi's talents were not widely recognised in academic circles, and he suffered a severe personal setback when in quick succession his wife and his two young children died. But his opera *Nabucco* ('Nebuchadnezzar') was a big success, and Verdi confidently wrote of it, 'With this opera my career as a composer may be said to have begun'. Not all his subsequent operas were so immediately successful, but from the first production of *Nabucco* until his death nearly sixty years later, Verdi was the unchallenged master of Italian opera. His most famous works include *Rigoletto*, based on a novel by Victor Hugo; *Il Trovatore* ('The Troubadour'); *La Traviata* ('The Woman Gone Astray'), based on a novel by Alexandre Dumas; *Simon Boccanegra*, named after its hero, a Doge of Genoa; *La Forza del Destino* ('The Force of Destiny'); *Don Carlos*, the hero in this case being the son of Philip II of Spain; and *Aida*. This last opera was intended to celebrate the opening of the Suez Canal in 1869, and is set in Egypt at the time of the pharaohs.

It is opera at its most spectacular, with sets and scenes conceived on the grandest scale.

Verdi was nearly sixty when *Aida* was first produced, but what many people regard as his two greatest operas were still to be composed. These are both based on plays by Shakespeare, and are the result of another of opera's famous collaborations between a composer and a librettist. The librettist in this case was Arrigo Boito, who had already written operas of his own. The first of their Shakespearian adaptations was *Otello*, and the second, completed when Verdi was eighty years old, was *Falstaff*, named after the principal character in the play *The Merry Wives of Windsor*. (This play had given its name to an earlier and very popular opera by the German composer Otto Nicolai). In his *Otello* and *Falstaff* Verdi came closest to Wagner's idea of music drama, whereby music, words and dramatic action are so tightly bound together that there is no place for the traditional type of aria.

Giacomo Puccini (1858–1924) is generally regarded as Verdi's successor, and while the artists in his opera *La Bohème* may have gone hungry in their Paris garret, Puccini himself became a very wealthy man. This opera and his other great successes, *Tosca* and *Madame Butterfly*, all contain famous arias, and Puccini is best known for his soaring passionate melodies. In fact, he used this gift quite sparingly, so that his big arias, when they do occur, are all the more effective. Equally effective was his ability to capture exactly the right dramatic atmosphere through his orchestration. In his last opera, *Turandot*, completed after his death by the composer Franco Alfano, he evokes in this way the dazzling colour and brilliance of imperial Peking at the time of the legendary Chinese Princess Turandot.

Puccini also contributed to a type of Italian opera called *verismo*, meaning 'truthful' or 'realistic' in the sense of bringing realism to bear on the sadder or more sordid facts of life. His opera *Il Tabarro* ('The Cloak') deals with jealousy and murder on board a canal barge. It is one of three one-act operas collectively known as *Il Trittico* ('The Triptych'). The other two are *Suor Angelica* ('Sister Angelica') and *Gianni Schicchi*, a comic opera.

Two other composers who contributed to the *verismo* type of opera were Ruggiero Leoncavallo (1858–1919) and Pietro Mascagni (1863–1945). Leoncavallo composed *Pagliacci* ('Clowns'),

Madame Butterfly, the tragic Japanese heroine of Puccini's opera. Oriental subjects attracted many composers, artists and writers around the turn of the century

which describes the real life drama of a group of actors. Mascagni wrote *Cavalleria Rusticana* ('Rustic Chivalry'), a story of love and revenge in Sicily. Each opera represents its composer's one big claim to fame, and because each is relatively short they are often performed on the same operatic bill.

Leoncavallo also composed an opera called *La Bohème*, though his work was eclipsed by Puccini's version. Another Italian composer, Ferruccio Busoni (1866–1924), wrote an opera called *Turandot*, which also failed to achieve the popularity of Puccini's own opera of that name. Busoni wrote other operas, but his greatest success was as a pianist and teacher. He loved particularly the music of J. S. Bach and made many arrangements of his works for the piano or the orchestra.

Ottorino Respighi (1879–1936) wrote operas, but had a similar love for the music of past ages. He composed one orchestral suite called *The Birds*, based on music of the 17th and 18th centuries. But he also had a fine gift for orchestration which he displayed to the full in two vividly descriptive companion pieces called *The Fountains of Rome* and *The Pines of Rome*.

Verdi was closely associated with the *Risorgimento*—the political and military movement aimed at winning the Italian-speaking provinces of the north from the empire of Austro-Hungary and creating a unified and independent kingdom of Italy. Indeed, he was almost as much of a national hero as Giuseppe Garibaldi, the patriot who led and won the military campaigns. The well-known chorus of Hebrew slaves from *Nabucco* was widely identified with the desire of the Italians to be free from foreign domination, and in several of his other operas Verdi ran into difficulties with the censors because they suspected a hidden political meaning in the plot. Verdi's own name was used as a political slogan—*Viva Verdi*—and there certainly was a hidden meaning to this. For the letters of the composer's name also stood for a forbidden slogan—*Viva Emmanuale re d'Italia* ('Long Live King Emmanuel of Italy'), the intended monarch of a sovereign Italian state.

During the same period, Wagner strongly supported the cause of German unity, achieved under the leadership of Bismarck after the Franco-Prussian war of 1870–1871. And in addition to all its other qualities, his opera *Die Meistersinger von Nürnberg* was intended to fill the German people with pride in their great cultural heritage.

Nationalism in music—the idea of writing music which in some way expresses the aspirations, character or spirit of a particular nation—was something that developed during the 19th century, when the modern political map of Europe was gradually taking shape. Composers of earlier times, like Bach, Couperin, Vivaldi or Purcell, wrote in styles which could be identified with German, French, Italian or English musical traditions, but such traditions were almost entirely confined to the art of music itself and had little or nothing to do with the expression of any broader national feeling. Beethoven and Schumann were two composers who started to use their native language for musical expressions and directions, instead of using the conventional Italian words and phrases, as a patriotic gesture. Weber was a hero of the 'Young German' movement of his day, and composed songs of a patriotic nature. Chopin and Liszt brought a strong element of patriotism to their music by quoting from Polish and Hungarian folk songs and dances. Liszt, as a Hungarian, felt that the culture of his native land was of great importance, and at the end of his life returned to Budapest to preside over the new Hungarian Academy of Music.

Bedřich Smetana (1824–1884) and Antonín Dvořák (1841–1904) committed themselves to the cause of Czech national independence through their music. One of Smetana's largest works is called, simply, *Ma Vlast* ('My Country'). It is a group of orchestral symphonic poems portraying different aspects of the life and landscape of his native land. In his comic opera *The Bartered Bride* Smetana made use of Czech folk dances and songs. Dvořák's best known works outside his own country are his Slavonic Dances, his Cello Concerto in B minor—one of the few great concertos for that instrument—and his symphonies. Dvořák was a fine late 19th century symphonist who shared with Brahms a mastery of classical symphonic form, and combined this with music that is generally warm and lyrical in spirit. The last of his symphonies, the Ninth in E minor, he composed while on a visit to the United States and has the subtitle 'From the New World'. This 'New World' Symphony contains melodies inspired by Negro spirituals, a feature of the music which expresses both Dvořák's interest in folk music everywhere and his deep sympathy for oppressed minorities.

Leoš Janáček (1854–1928) was another Czech nationalist composer. He made a study of the special inflections of Czech speech declaring that 'a fragment of national life is attached to every word uttered by the people'. He then re-created these speech sounds in his music. Janáček wrote many of his best works during the last years of his life, when he was inspired by his love for a young woman. He composed a string quartet to which he gave the title *Intimate Letters* because it contains passages which sound very much as though he were reading out a love letter. Janáček also composed several operas. One of these is *The Cunning Little Vixen*, an allegory about the life of a fox, in which he similarly expresses the sounds of nature in musical terms.

Spain was one of the oldest sovereign states in Europe, so the question of national independence and unity did not arise as it had done in Italy, Germany or Czechoslovakia. Nevertheless, Spanish composers became just as interested in the creation of a national style or school of music as their colleagues elsewhere. The founder figure of this movement was Felipe Pedrell (1841–1922), who edited and revived much old Spanish music, as well as composing operas and other works of his own. But it was his successors whose music is now most often heard outside Spain itself. Isaac Albéniz (1860–1909), Enrique Granados (1867–1916) and Joaquín Turina (1882–1949) all modelled their own music—mainly songs and piano pieces—on Spanish folk songs and dances. Granados wrote a set of piano pieces called *Goyescas*, inspired by the paintings of his fellow countryman Francisco Goya, the best known of these being entitled 'The Maiden and the Nightingale'. Shortly afterwards he used some of the music again in an opera bearing the same title.

Manuel de Falla (1876–1946) is regarded by many people as the greatest Spanish composer. He was born in the southern province of Andalusia, home of flamenco singing and dancing. This very distinctive and exciting type of folk music grew out of an earlier folk music tradition called *cante hondo*, literally meaning 'deep song' and describing a very sad, even tragic kind of singing. The performance of flamenco music also includes certain Arabic words and exclamations, a reminder that Spain was occupied by the Moors of North Africa during the Middle Ages. Falla loved this

Spanish flamenco dancers

music, and its rhythms, melodies and harmonies run through much of the music which he himself composed. His principal works are the opera *La vida breve* ('Life is Short'), the ballet scores *The Three-Cornered Hat* and *El Amor brujo* ('Love, the Magician')—the latter containing the well known 'Ritual Fire Dance' —*Nights in the Gardens of Spain* for piano and orchestra, and a group of specially arranged Spanish folk songs.

Spain and Portugal between them colonised almost the whole of central and south America during the renaissance period, and their cultural influence remains very strong. In the realm of music both Manuel Ponce (1882–1948) in Mexico and Heitor Villa-Lobos (1887–1959) in Brazil have composed many pieces for that most Spanish of all instruments, the guitar. Villa-Lobos also wrote a substantial group of instrumental pieces called *Bachianas Brasileiras* which combine images of Brazilian life and folk music with some of the musical styles and forms of J. S. Bach. One of these pieces is subtitled 'The Little Train of Caipira' and paints a picture in sound of a little steam train wending its way across the hot, dusty Brazilian countryside. Other Latin American composers have been interested in the art and music of the American Indians, the inhabitants of the continent before the Spanish and Portuguese arrived. Carlos Chavez (born 1899), another Mexican composer, has written music for Aztec instruments, the Aztecs being the original inhabitants of Mexico. Alberto Ginastera (born 1916) in Argentina has written music for a ballet which is based on an American Indian legend.

Another important group of composers inspired by the traditions and ideals of their homeland came from the countries of Scandinavia. In Norway, Edvard Hagerup Grieg (1843–1907) based nearly all his music on the folk songs and dances of his native country. When a fellow musician said that one of his compositions was too Norwegian, Grieg replied, 'On the contrary. The next one will be even more so!' He wrote many songs and piano pieces, but his most popular composition is his one relatively large-scale work for the concert hall, the Piano Concerto in A minor. Grieg also wrote some very fine incidental music to the play *Peer Gynt* by Norway's greatest dramatist, Henrick Ibsen.

Finland had long felt itself threatened by Russia, its giant neighbour to the east, and like the Poles who had similarly endured centuries of domination by more powerful neighbours, the Finns were intensely patriotic. Their greatest composer, Jean Sibelius (1865–1957), gave voice to this patriotism in an early work called *Finlandia*, which became almost like a second national anthem. But Sibelius went on to express the spirit and character of his homeland in much more imaginative ways. Finnish myths and legends inspired him to compose symphonic poems such as *The Swan of Tuonela* and *Tapiola*, which evoke a world of dark, silent forests and lakes, or of raging wind and snow. Most impressive of all are his violin concerto and his seven symphonies. Through these Sibelius gradually perfected a very original symphonic style, condensing and compressing his material until it sounds as solid and strong as a rock.

Carl Nielsen (1865–1931), generally regarded as Denmark's greatest composer, and an exact contemporary of Sibelius, wrote another impressive group of symphonies. Some of these have interesting names. The Second Symphony is called *The Four Temperaments*. This title refers to the medieval classification of the four types of human personality—choleric, phlegmatic, melancholic, sanguine—which provide a basis for the work's four movements. The Fourth Symphony bears the title *The Inextinguishable* (or 'Unquenchable'), and expresses Nielsen's own belief that 'Music is life, and as such is unquenchable'. A significant technical feature of these works is their *progressive tonality*, meaning that they start in one key and end in another. Mahler also used progressive tonality in some of his symphonies.

English musical life since Handel's time had been strongly influenced by Germans, partly because English kings and queens were of German descent and favoured German musicians. In the 19th century Mendelssohn was a particular favourite of Queen Victoria and her German consort Prince Albert, and loved by English audiences. He wrote his oratorio *Elijah* for the Birmingham Music Festival, one of the most important in Europe and famous for the quality of the choral singing.

Arthur Sullivan (1842–1900) came under this German influence as much as any other English musician of the period, but through his symphony and other orchestral and choral works he greatly helped to re-establish the name of English music abroad, although he himself was of Irish-Italian-Jewish descent. He is best remembered today for such comic operettas as *H.M.S Pinafore, Iolanthe* and *The Mikado* which he wrote in collaboration with the librettist W. S. Gilbert. The 'Gilbert and Sullivan' operas have for a long time been phenomenally popular in English-speaking countries, including the United States.

Edward Elgar (1857–1934) also became a figure of international stature, and in his own country he is generally considered to be the greatest English-born composer since Purcell. One of the works which helped Elgar to win recognition after years of obscurity and disappointment was his *Enigma Variations*, the usual form of title given to his 'Variations on an Original Theme', in which each variation is also a musical portrait of one of the composer's friends. The 'enigma' refers to the theme itself, which Elgar said provided a counterpoint to a well known tune. Scholars now believe this tune is 'Auld lang syne', although Elgar never revealed his secret.

During the First World War, Elgar also became something of a national hero when words were added to the theme from one of his set of orchestral marches called *Pomp and Circumstance*. It then became a patriotic hymn called 'Land of Hope and Glory'. Elgar, however, did not write the words, and like most artists who lived through it, the war deeply depressed him and affected his work. But by then he had composed most of his other major works, including the oratorio *The Dream of Gerontius*, a violin concerto and two majestic-sounding symphonies. None of Elgar's compositions makes direct use of English folk music, but they all express his deep love of England, both of the countryside and of Edwardian London, capital city of what was still the greatest empire in the world.

Other musicians of Elgar's generation did take up a serious study of English folk music. Cecil Sharp collected and edited many such traditional folk songs and dances, just as Bartók and Kodály (discussed later) were doing in their own country, and although he composed little music himself, his work in this field inspired other English composers. Ralph Vaughan Williams (1872–1958) made people realise how beautiful much of this English folk music was with such orchestral arrangements as *Fantasia on Greensleeves*, and set to music poems about rural England, such as his song cycle *On Wenlock Edge* to poems by A. E. Housman. Vaughan Williams also drew attention to great English music of earlier times in works like *Fantasia on a Theme by Thomas Tallis*. Gustav Holst (1874–1934) shared Vaughan Williams' love of English folk music, and several of his own compositions have a folk music basis. But Holst was equally interested in mysticism and the occult, and this interest prompted his best known work, the orchestral suite *The Planets*. Each of the movements is inspired by the astrological character attached to the different planets, and the last—'Neptune, the Mystic'—includes some very imaginative writing for women's voices. Frederick Delius (1862–1934) based his orchestral work *An English Rhapsody: Brigg Fair* on an old Lincolnshire folk song introduced to him by his friend Percy Grainger, and in this and some other compositions many English listeners feel that Delius came very close to capturing in music the spirit of the English countryside. He did not, however, share with Vaughan Williams, Holst, Grainger and others their deep interest in English folk music. Delius's father was German, and although he himself was born and brought up in England, he spent most of his adult life abroad, developing a style that owed very little to any other musical school or movement of his time.

The most impressive of all nationalist schools of music was that which grew up in Russia. Until the 19th century, Imperial Russia had contributed little to the art and culture of Europe. Russian tsars like Peter the Great admired the art and architecture of other European countries and copied such styles in their own country. At other times in her history, Russia, a country of immense distances and vast, impenetrable forests, stretching eastwards and south-wards into Asia, withdrew almost completely from European affairs. Then, early in the 19th century, came a succession of Russian writers and musicians who were among the greatest creative men of their age, and who in turn influenced the course of Western literature and music.

In literature the first great writer was Alexander Pushkin, who was followed by such major novelists and dramatists as Nicolai Gogol, Feodor Dostoevsky, Leo Tolstoy and Anton Chekhov. In music the corresponding figure to Pushkin was Mikhail Glinka (1804–1857). His two outstanding works were his operas *Ivan Sussasnin*, also known as *A Life for the Tsar*, based on the life of a 17th century Russian peasant hero, and *Russlan and Ludmilla*. After him came a group of five composers, known as 'The Five' or 'The Mighty Handful', who worked closely together, dedicating themselves to the creation of a national school of music inspired by Russian folk music, history and legend. These five composers were Mily Balakirev (1837–1910), César Cui (1835–1918), Modest Mussorgsky (1839–1881), Alexander Borodin (1833–1887) and

Nicolai Rimsky-Korsakov (1844–1908). One other interesting point these five men had in common was that none of them was a completely professional musician. Borodin, for example, was a chemist, Mussorgsky had been an army officer, and Rimsky-Korsakov had served in the navy.

Rimsky-Korsakov, Borodin and Mussorgsky are the best known members of the Five today. Rimsky-Korsakov was a master of orchestration, as he displayed in his opera *The Golden Cockerel*, based on a work by Pushkin, and in his set of four pieces described as a symphonic suite, *Schéhérazade*. This composition was inspired by 'Tales from the Arabian Nights', and Rimsky-Korsakov wrote some very effective and atmospheric music to describe the magic and adventure of the stories.

Borodin wrote two symphonies, some chamber music and songs, but his most popular work is his opera *Prince Igor*, containing the Polovtsian Dances. Borodin died before he had finished the opera. Rimsky-Korsakov, who saw himself as a kind of father figure of the Five, completed the work, then revised and edited the whole score.

Mussorgsky had a particularly strong feeling for the spirit of Russian folk music, and some people think he was the most original and naturally gifted of the Five. He wrote some remarkable songs, a symphonic poem *Night on the Bare Mountain*, and one of the most colourful and dramatic of Russian operas, *Boris Godunov*, based on events in Russian history. Once again, Rimsky-Korsakov, who thought that Mussorgsky's own orchestration and harmonization were rather untutored, undertook a revision of the score of both works. Mussorgsky's other major composition is a group of pieces called *Pictures at an Exhibition*. This work is a famous example of programme music. Each picture is vividly depicted by its own piece of music, while the work as a whole is unified by a recurring theme which describes the leisurely progress of a visitor to the exhibition, who stops to look at each picture in turn. Mussorgsky wrote this work for the piano, but Ravel later orchestrated it, and this is the version most often played today.

Most celebrated of all the Russian composers was Peter Tchaikovsky (1840–1893). He sympathised with the nationalist feelings of the Five, though he never felt close enough to them in

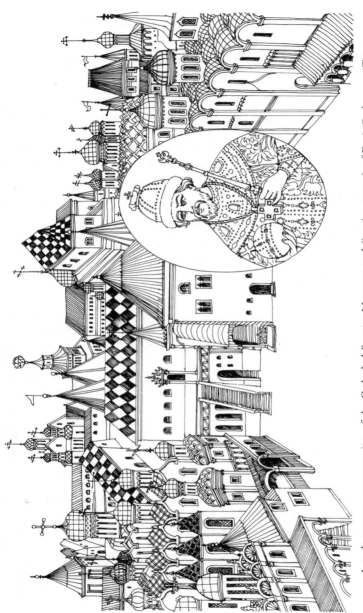

A 17th century representation of the Cathedral Square, Moscow, and (inset) a portrait of Boris Godunov as Tsar

spirit to be a member of their group. By contrast, Tchaikovsky was a thoroughly professional musician with a broad knowledge of the music of many foreign composers, so that most of his own music has a much more cosmopolitan sound to it than the work of the Five. Indeed, Tchaikovsky's music soon became popular all over the world, and he himself travelled a good deal, conducting performances of his music in Europe and America, though he did not enjoy such publicity.

The features that people love in Tchaikovsky's music are the big, sweeping melodies and his dramatic and vivid orchestration. He displayed these qualities to the full in a fairly early work, the symphonic poem, or fantasy-overture as he called it, *Romeo and Juliet*, which brilliantly sums up in music the story of Shakespeare's play. He went on to write music for almost every established musical form: six symphonies, four piano concertos, a violin concerto, sets of variations, orchestral suites, songs and chamber music; and for the stage such operas as *Eugene Onegin* and *The Queen of Spades*, both based on works by Pushkin, and his three great ballet scores.

The traditional home of ballet had been France ever since the time of Louis XIV and the operas of Lully with their love of spectacle and dancing. French operas from then on almost always included a big ballet sequence, and the French language was, and still is, used to describe the dance steps and other stage movements of classical ballet. In the 19th century French composers, besides writing ballet music as a part of their operas, also wrote the music for full-length ballet productions. Chief among these were Leo Delibes (1836–1891) with *Coppélia* and Adolphe Adam (1803–1856) with *Giselle*. But it was Tchaikovsky, a Russian, who achieved the greatest fame and popularity with his three ballets *Swan Lake*, *The Sleeping Beauty* and *The Nutcracker*.

Tchaikovsky was a very emotional man, and another feature of much of his music is the way it conveys his own moods and feelings. This typically romantic attitude to his work he described in detail in the letters he wrote to various friends, among whom was Madame Nadezhda von Meck, a rich widow who liked his music and supported him financially for many years. In one letter containing information about his Sixth Symphony in B minor (*Pathétique*) he wrote: 'A symphony with a programme, but a

The ballerinas in the first production of *Swan Lake* in 1877

programme that will remain an enigma to all. Often while composing it in my mind I shed tears.'

This symphony contains passages of the deepest melancholy and others of wild excitement. Tchaikovsky made great use of dynamics to increase the dramatic force of the music. At one point in the score he indicated 'ppppp', meaning as quietly as possible, almost to the point of inaudibility. This passage is followed immediately by another marked 'ff', in order to achieve the most arresting change of mood. Before the 19th century, composers rarely marked any passage of music beyond 'p' for *piano* or 'f' for *forte*. Beethoven greatly increased the dramatic power of music, and at one point in the last movement of his Seventh Symphony in A major called for the orchestra to play a chord 'fff'. Tchaikovsky's extreme use of dynamics showed how much expression romantic composers wanted their music to convey. Such demands also showed how music had reached a peak of orchestral discipline and virtuosity by the end of the 19th century.

A Russian composer who was also a famous pianist was Alexander Scriabin (1872–1915). What makes him interesting today was his own interest in theosophy, a kind of occult religion something like spiritualism, which had a big following in Europe and America towards the end of the 19th century. Occultism of one sort or another interested many writers, artists and some other musicians at about this time. Scriabin's involvement with theosophy led him to compose a number of works, including *Prometheus, The Poem of Fire*, for piano and orchestra, based on a special chord which he called the 'mystic chord'. Scriabin also thought of special lighting effects for the performance of this work.

Sergei Rachmaninov (1873–1943), an even more celebrated pianist–composer, was another of those influenced by the occultism of his time. He wrote a symphonic poem called *The Isle of the Dead*, prompted by the painting of a strange Swiss–German artist named Arnold Böcklin, and he set to music for chorus and orchestra a poem called *The Bells* by the American Edgar Allen Poe, who wrote many stories about the macabre and the supernatural. The general romantic, melancholy character of Rachmaninov's music is evident in his piano preludes, symphonies, piano concertos and *Rhapsody on a Theme of Paganini* for piano and orchestra; and though he never returned to his homeland after he had settled in the United States, Rachmaninov continued throughout his life to write many songs and other choral pieces inspired by Russian folk music.

The various ways in which composers identified themselves with their own countries led to significant new developments in the art of music during the early years of the 20th century. Béla Bartók (1881–1945) and Zoltán Kodály (1882–1967) in Hungary studied the folk music of their native land and of neighbouring countries like Romania. An interest in folk music by composers of so-called 'serious music' was by no means unknown before the nationalist period. Haydn, who was born and brought up among the peasants of Croatia, loved their music and frequently used its tunes and rhythms in his trios, quartets and symphonies. But nobody before Bartók and Kodály had made such a truly scientific inquiry into the subject and then so thoroughly absorbed the special rhythms, melodies and colours of Hungarian and Romanian folk songs and dances into their own music.

Hungarian hurdy-gurdy player and dancer in traditional costume

Kodály's most popular composition is an orchestral suite based on the music from his opera *Háry János*. It opens humorously with an orchestral 'sneeze'. According to Hungarian custom, any story that starts with a sneeze should not be taken too seriously. Bartók, especially, recognised that the unique strength and power of his native folk music lay precisely in its tough, elemental character, and he was determined to preserve this. Bartók himself was extremely shy and gentle, but to many of his contemporaries, still used to the rich harmonies and orchestration of 19th century composers, he must sometimes have seemed, through his music, to be a fierce and barbaric person. One interesting feature of this music is *polytonality*—'many tones'. This means writing a piece of music in two or more keys at the same time, the effect being to release the music from the conventional rules of the twenty-four major and minor keys. Today Bartók's piano works, his six string quartets—regarded by many as the finest group of such works since Beethoven—and orchestral compositions like Music for Strings, Percussion and Celeste, are seen as most influential to the development of 20th century music, as well as being beautiful works in their own right. Bartók also wrote a few most unusual works for the stage, notably his opera *Duke Bluebeard's Castle*, which explores the psychology of the legendary character who murdered his wives.

In France Claude-Achille Debussy (1862–1918) was also anxious to escape from the existing conventions of harmony and to create a musical style that would express his own personality and stand for his country. There had been many eminent 19th century French composers before him. Besides Berlioz, who was rather neglected by his own countrymen, there were Charles Gounod (1818–1893) and Jules Massenet (1842–1912), both very successful operatic composers. French opera in the 19th century still followed the general pattern of opera established at the time of Lully with plenty of spectacle, big set pieces for the chorus and a ballet sequence. Gounod's *Faust*, an outstanding example of this type of opera, was immensely popular all over Europe and America during the composer's own lifetime. Georges Bizet (1838–1875) composed the music to *Carmen*, an opera making brilliant use of the drama and spectacle of the Spanish bull-ring, and this has become one of the most successful operas of all time, although Bizet did not live long enough to see this come about.

Camille Saint-Saëns (1835–1921) was an equally eminent composer of symphonies, concertos and other orchestral and instrumental works, including his humorous *Le Carnaval des animaux* ('Carnival of the Animals'). César Franck (1822–1890), Belgian by birth, spent most of his life in Paris as an organist, but late in his career wrote several instrumental and orchestral works of distinction. Gabriel Fauré (1845–1924) composed much fine chamber music, a particularly beautiful setting of the Requiem Mass, and helped to establish a style of French song (or *chanson*) comparable to that of the German *Lied*.

Despite these achievements, Debussy was very conscious of the dominating influence of German music, and this acted as a spur to his efforts to create a new musical 'language' or 'idiom'. As a student he already held some very strong and individual views about harmony, frequently arguing with his teachers over the text-book rules concerning harmonic modulation and the way one chord should lead to another. Debussy contended that each chord was a fascinating thing in itself and should not be tied to any particular set of rules. He also took a keen interest in some of the scales used in oriental music, and in the old church modes, believing that he could make something quite new out of them.

The new and very original musical style which Debussy evolved coincided with an equally novel style in architecture and design, also centred on France, called *art nouveau* ('new art'). But the general character of his music is more often compared with a slightly earlier artistic movement called Impressionism. French artists like Edgar Degas, Auguste Renoir and Claude Monet had painted what they considered to be impressions of scenes as conveyed to them by particular qualities of light and shade. They formed the Impressionist School of painting. Debussy similarly created impressions of places or scenes in many of his compositions.

Debussy's first important orchestral work was *Prélude à l'Après-midi d'un faune* ('Prelude to the Afternoon of a Faun'), suggesting the feelings of physical luxury of a beautiful young creature on a warm summer's day. His next orchestral composition was a group of three pieces called *Nocturnes*, the first of these bearing the very impressionistic title of *Nuages* ('Clouds'). Debussy's most substantial orchestral work, *La Mer* ('The Sea'), depicts the sea in all its moods, from flat calm to raging storm. This work, subtitled 'Three Symphonic Sketches', displays most fully its composer's very subtle and refined style of orchestration. *Ibéria*, by contrast, vividly suggests the heat and light of Spain.

In *Pelléas et Mélisande* Debussy brought to the opera house sounds and images as new and subtle as those he introduced into the concert hall. This, his only opera, was based on a play by the Belgian dramatist and poet Maurice Maeterlinck about a legendary kingdom of long ago, similar, in time and place, to that depicted in Wagner's *Tristan und Isolde*. But in contrast to the emotional intensity of Wagner's music drama, Debussy's music dwells upon the shifting twilight of a dense forest, where much of the action takes place, while the characters themselves seem to exist, for most of the time, in a kind of dream.

Debussy's other best known compositions are those for the solo piano. The piano had reached its ultimate state of technical refinement by the early years of the 20th century, and Debussy extracted from the instrument subtleties and intricacies of tone which not even Liszt had dreamed of. Debussy's most significant group of piano compositions are two sets of preludes, applying the word, as Chopin did, to pieces which are complete in themselves. Nearly all these preludes bear an impressionistic title, such as *Le vent dans la plaine* ('Wind over the Plain'), *Brouillards* ('Mists'), *Feux d'artifice* ('Fireworks'), and each marvellously captures its particular image or impression. However, editions of the printed music do not carry these titles at the head of each piece. They are printed at the end, in parenthesis, as though Debussy was reluctant to attach specific images to pieces which contain some of his most advanced and rarified musical thoughts.

Debussy's name is often linked with that of his compatriot Maurice Ravel (1875–1937). Ravel did compose some very fine impressionistic music, mainly for the piano, including *Jeux d'eau* ('Play of the Water'), and a group of pieces called *Miroirs* ('Mirrors'). But there were sides to his character, as a person and as an artist, which led him to develop a musical personality quite distinct from that of Debussy. Ravel loved the world of fantasy and make-believe, which he expressed in such works as the ballet *Ma mère l'oye* ('Mother Goose'), inspired by the fairy tales of Charles Perrault, and the one-act opera *L'Enfant et les sortilèges*, about a small boy whose toys come suddenly to life. Ravel also wrote much more music than Debussy in established forms, like the string quartet, trio and piano concerto, or music with some particular reference to past styles. *Le tombeau de Couperin* ('Couperin's Tomb') is a kind of homage to the great French composer of the baroque period, and consists of a group of pieces modelled on the various dance forms of Couperin's day. At the same time, the adventurous harmonies and very polished, almost transparently clear sound of these pieces make them perfect examples of Ravel's own style.

Above all, Ravel was one of the greatest masters of orchestration. His usual practice was first to write a piece of music for the

Ondine, the water sprite, the title of a piano piece by both Debussy and Ravel. The movement and properties of water fascinated impressionist painters and composers

piano and then to orchestrate it. Thus many of his compositions exist in two versions, and to compare them gives the listener a fascinating insight into the art of orchestration as practised by Ravel. His largest orchestral work, however, was always conceived as such. It is the score to the ballet *Daphnis et Chloé*, which includes a large chorus in addition to an orchestra of more than a hundred players. The ballet is set in a mythical Greek landscape, and the best known passage from the score depicts dawn and sunrise. This is a superb example of what is sometimes called tone painting in music. Even a person who knew nothing about the ballet could hardly mistake the music for anything other than an evocation of the first glimmer of light on the horizon, the awakening of the birds and the final appearance of the sun itself, flooding the sky with gold.

Debussy and Ravel, like Bartók, created styles which carried music away from the late romantic 'richness' of German-speaking composers like Wagner, Bruckner and Richard Strauss. Other French composers, at about the time of the First World War, were even more determined to escape from the influence of German music, with its emphasis on the growth and structure of musical ideas and forms. They wished to re-assert the traditional French qualities of eloquence and clarity—qualities especially associated with the French language. Eric Satie (1866–1925) was a leading figure in this movement. He wrote some music which is most graceful, restrained and subtle, and other pieces with eccentric titles or effects, deliberately intended to shake his audiences out of the serious state of mind in which they listened to Beethoven, Brahms or Wagner. Satie and the writer and artist Jean Cocteau brought together a younger group of composers who called themselves *Les Six*. Their declared aim was to write music which was light, clear and uncomplicated. The three best known members of *Les Six* are Arthur Honegger (1892–1955), who was Swiss by birth, Francis Poulenc (1899–1963) and Darius Milhaud (1892–1975). At one time Honegger was very well known for a piece of orchestral music called *Pacific 231* which evokes the sound and motion of a railway steam locomotive.

However, the man who attempted the most complete and dramatic break with the past was the Austrian-born composer Arnold Schoenberg (1874–1951). He started by writing some of the weightiest of all music in the post-Wagnerian style. His *Gurrelieder* ('Songs of Gurra') is a mammoth work for four solo singers, four separate choruses and a huge orchestra, and the music is filled with dark and heavy emotion. Indeed, it was compositions like this that made Schoenberg feel he had come to a musical dead end and must seek some new direction for his work. So, after much thought, he began to reconstruct music on the basis of a new type of scale called a *tone-row*. The scales of the twenty-four major and minor keys, on which Western music had been based for over three hundred years, each contain eight notes, these conforming to a tonal structure which gives each note within a given scale a special relationship with the other seven. Schoenberg's tone-rows included, in various arrangements, all twelve notes of the chromatic scale (the black and white notes on a piano keyboard between any note and the same note an octave above or below), and these were free of any particular tonal relationship. Music based on such principles sounded fundamentally different from anything heard before, as might any language based on a new kind of alphabet.

Schoenberg's revolutionary new kind of music is known as *twelve-tone* music, or, using the equivalent Greek word, *dodecaphonic* music. People sometimes also call it *serial* music, because it employs a special series of notes (though this term can apply to other musical techniques); and in the broadest context it comes under the heading of *atonal* music, meaning that it is free from the tonalities of the established major and minor keys and scales. For a long time this twelve-tone music bewildered and perplexed not only concert-goers but many professional musicians, as did Schoenberg's development of a new method of singing called *Sprechgesang* ('speech-song'). In this, the vocalist follows the pitch of a sequence of notes but does not sustain the pitch from one note to the next as he or she would in a normal song, thus creating the effect of hovering somewhere between speaking and singing. Schoenberg's most celebrated use of *Sprechgesang* comes in a song-cycle with the French title *Pierrot lunaire* ('Moonstruck Pierrot'). The strange, dream-like quality of this composition is a reminder that Sigmund Freud and other pioneers of modern psychology were at that time inquiring into the nature of dreams and of the unconscious or subconscious mind. Other creative people, such as the painters Max Ernst and Salvador Dali, and the writer James Joyce, also explored these aspects of psychology in their work.

Schoenberg had two pupils who developed twelve-tone music in their own way. They were Anton Webern (1883–1945) and Alban Berg (1885–1935). The three composers together formed what is often referred to as the Second Viennese School, as distinct from those earlier composers—Mozart, Beethoven, Schubert, Brahms—who had all lived and worked in Vienna and created a musical tradition of their own. The main feature of Webern's music is its extreme concentration. Webern used notes with great deliberation, attaching something of the same kind of significance to individual notes and tones as did the painter Piet Mondrian to rectangles of colour and straight lines. In Webern's case the effect was to make his compositions very brief. One of his Five Pieces for Orchestra lasts for only nineteen seconds.

Berg wrote much larger-scale works, including two operas, *Wozzeck* and *Lulu*, and a violin concerto, a very expressive piece of music prompted by the death of a friend.

Musicians not directly associated with the so-called Second Viennese School have also concentrated on twelve-tone methods of composition. Two of these are the Italian composers Luigi Dallapiccola (1904–1975) and Luigi Nono (born 1924).

While Schoenberg was reshaping the techniques of musical composition, another kind of music, totally opposite in style and character, was making rapid headway. This was jazz, and the features of jazz, in one form or another, have become as familiar to most people today as the motor car and the radio.

The origins of jazz are bound up with the story of the African Negroes who were shipped across the Atlantic ocean to work as slaves on the cotton plantations of the southern states of the United States of America. Their story is a terrible one. Some of them did not survive the ocean crossing. The majority of those who did were condemned to a life of hardship and poverty. But they could not be deprived of their music which, like all true folk music, was as fundamental and natural a part of their lives as eating and sleeping. They sang in the fields to sustain themselves during the long hours of back-breaking work. They sang of their sorrows and miseries, and about their simple faith in the joys and rewards of heaven.

The outstanding feature of this music was rhythm—that aspect of music which people everywhere respond to more readily than to any other means of communication. The American Negroes' acute sense of rhythm came directly from the dances of their African homeland, and it dominated every bar of their own music. The other significant feature was improvisation—something common to all folk music. They had various kinds of song which everybody grew up with, but because these were seldom if ever written down or remembered in any other systematic way, they were recreated on each occasion according to mood and inclination.

The event which changed the lives of millions of American Negroes was President Abraham Lincoln's emancipation of the slaves at the end of the American Civil War of 1861–1865. Large numbers of the Negro population then left the plantations—many of which had been ruined by the war—and moved into the towns and cities of the South, and especially to New Orleans, principal port of the cotton trade. This city and the surrounding areas had a large French or half-French population dating from the 17th and 18th centuries when French settlers had colonised the whole of the Mississippi valley from the Great Lakes down to the Gulf of Mexico. The half-French people were called creoles, and many of them had a good understanding of European music. From the blending of creole musical tastes and Negro musical styles emerged the earliest forms of what was variously called 'jass', 'jasz' and, finally, jazz.

By 1900 there were several recognisable jazz forms. There were rags and stomps, bright, brash, lively pieces that inspired such classic jazz numbers as *Tiger Rag, King Porter Stomp* and *Sugar Foot Stomp*. But most famous and enduring was the music called blues. In this type of song, with its regularly repeated lines and basic jazz harmonies, black singers lamented the problems and hardships which were their common lot.

I can't make a nickel, I'm flat as can be,
Some people say money is talking, but it won't say a word to me

are the opening lines of the *Bad Time Blues*. Another famous blues number is *Tin Roof Blues*, suggesting the poverty-stricken home-steads of the old plantations.

Blues singers often just accompanied themselves on a banjo or even a mouth organ, moving from place to place much as the troubadours and minstrels of the Middle Ages had done. Other Negroes acquired instruments which had belonged to the numerous military bands of the Civil War period. They often formed street bands of their own, especially for funerals when they would accompany the mourners to and from the cemetery. Or they joined up with six or seven other musicians to form the earliest jazz bands. Such bands usually consisted of a 'front line' of trumpet, trombone or clarinet, which provided the melody; and a 'rhythm section' of drums and other percussion instruments, plus a banjo, guitar, double bass, or sousaphone. This massive brass wind instrument, which encircled the player's body and sounded very like a tuba, derived its name from John Philip Sousa (1854–1932), the American military band leader and composer of such famous marches as *The Washington Post* and *The Stars and Stripes Forever*.

W. C. Handy, Buddy Bolden, Joseph 'King' Oliver, Ferdinand 'Jelly Roll' Morton (whose real name was Ferdinand Joseph La Menthe), Sidney Bechet, Edward 'Kid' Ory and Louis Armstrong were jazz band leaders and instrumentalists who were already famous by the end of the First World War. Bessie Smith and Billie Holiday, two of the greatest black jazz singers, also grew up during this time. Bessie Smith was badly hurt in a road accident and may have died because she was refused admission to a 'white' hospital. Billie Holiday died prematurely of drink and drugs, like many other black musicians who were victims of the rough and sometimes brutal conditions in which they had to live and work. Both women expressed much of the sadness and tragedy of their own lives in their singing. Thomas 'Fats' Waller, by contrast, expressed the black man's exuberant spirit. His large, rolling eyes and jaunty bowler hat went perfectly with such celebrated numbers as *Ain't Misbehavin'* and *Honeysuckle Rose*.

As black people first moved from the country to the towns and cities of the South, so many of them then migrated to the industrial cities in the north in search of work. They took their music with them, and in this way jazz spread across the United States like a plant or tree growing upwards and outwards from its roots in and

A New Orleans street band. Note the mammoth sousaphone, inherited from American military bands

113

around New Orleans. The music itself changed and developed as well. A jazz piano style associated particularly with St Louis and Chicago was boogie woogie. This was like a speeded up version of the blues, with a distinctive part for the pianist's left hand. One of the pioneers of boogie was Charlie 'Cow Cow' Davenport, whose *Cow Cow Boogie* got its name from the cowcatcher attached to the front of American railway engines. During this time many poor black and white Americans travelled about the country by 'jumping' a lift on freight trains. Another famous boogie musician was Clarence 'Pine Top' Smith, shot dead in a dance hall fight. These and other boogie pianists often played at 'house-rent' parties—functions held by tenement dwellers to help them raise money to pay their rent. So-called 'bath tub' liquor was as typical of such parties as the music. This was the age of Prohibition in the United States, and people either had to buy 'boot-leg' beer or spirits from gangsters like Al Capone or make their own—in the bath tub.

A new and much more polished kind of jazz band was also created by musicians like Edward 'Duke' Ellington and William 'Count' Basie. They modified the structure of the basic New Orleans type of band, increased the number of players, and prepared compositions and arrangements of a high musical quality. One important feature of the bands of Duke Ellington and Count Basie was the saxophone section. The saxophone has a reed fitted to its mouthpiece like most woodwind instruments, but it is made of brass or some other metal (today it may be plastic). Its inventor, the 19th century Belgian instrument maker Adolphe Sax, designed it specially to give more power to the woodwind section in large French military bands. A few composers, including Bizet, have written parts for it in their orchestral scores, but the saxophone did not really capture the imagination of musicians until the jazz era. Band leaders like Ellington and Basie employed saxophones of various sizes producing different ranges of notes (e.g. alto, tenor, soprano), very similar to a set of recorders or viols in renaissance times.

During the 1920s, when Duke Ellington and Count Basie were forming their first bands, white Americans began seriously to take up jazz. One of the first and most gifted of these was Leon Bismarck 'Bix' Beiderbecke. His principal instrument was the cornet, but he was also a good pianist, and wrote a piano piece called *In a Mist*. This composition owes something to Debussy, a composer whose music has fascinated other jazz musicians, just as early jazz styles fascinated him. Ellington and Basie themselves were exponents of 'mainstream' jazz. Their music sounded much more professional and sophisticated than that of earlier jazz men; at the same time, it still clearly flowed from 'traditional' jazz styles. In the 1940s, though, new styles developed which carried jazz far from its origins. One of these was called rebop, or bebop. This word, often shortened to bop, was a way of describing the rather hectic character of the music. The two men who really established bebop were saxophonist Charlie Parker (known as 'Bird') and trumpeter Dizzy Gillespie. Both were highly original and deep thinking musicians who did not correspond in any way to the traditional image of the black man as a simple entertainer. Another special jazz style was created by, among others, trumpeter Miles Davis. The music he played was, by contrast, very cool and ethereal in sound, and became known as 'cool' jazz.

Such music, and the music of even more advanced, or 'progressive' jazz men, was too technical or intellectual to became really popular. But right back in the days of its infancy jazz had begun to influence popular styles of music. Before the First World War 'Nigger Minstrel Shows' were enjoyed by millions of white Americans and Europeans, who mistakenly believed such entertainment to be real jazz. By the end of the war the new, fashionable dances—notably the Charleston—all had certain jazz features, suitably modified for white people's tastes. Their most recognisable feature was *syncopation*. This means displacing the normal rhythmic beat of a piece of music in some way, perhaps by accenting a note between two normal beats or producing a kind of slur from one beat to the next. Syncopation was not new to music—Beethoven, for example, had often made use of it—but it quickly became identified with jazz or jazz-derived music. Scott Joplin wrote a number of piano pieces, such as *Maple Leaf Rag*, in a syncopated style. These were quite restrained and genteel and suitable for any drawing room, but the ragtime dances that followed were full of syncopated energy and bounce.

This syncopation broadened out into the most popular dance style of all—swing. The swing bands of the 1930s and 1940s were

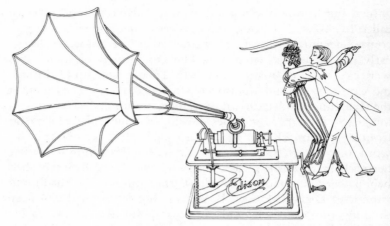

A phonograph of 1912. These and early gramophones did much to spread the popularity of dances like the Charleston and the Black Bottom

almost exclusively the creation of white musicians—they frequently included a string section, a type of instrumentation outside the experience of most black musicians. And radio, another creation of white Americans and Europeans, was the medium which carried their music into the homes of white people everywhere. Paul Whiteman, Artie Shaw, Benny Goodman, Woody Herman, Tommy Dorsey and Glenn Miller were the most celebrated swing band leaders. Even more famous were some of the vocalists who performed with them, such as Bing Crosby and the young Frank Sinatra.

After the Second World War the big swing bands gradually went out of fashion, and in their place came much smaller instrumental groups whose music was perhaps closer to the early spirit of jazz. This was rock n' roll, so called because it described the movements of those who danced to it. Rock n' roll, like boogie, was another speeded up version of the blues, played with great vigour, usually with electrically amplified guitars supported by a strong and emphatic rhythm section. This style of music, made immensely popular by singers like Elvis Presley, was, in its turn, followed by what was actually called popular, or pop music. The most successful pop group of the 1960s was The Beatles. They formed their group of four in Liverpool, and were among the very few European musicians, since the conception of jazz, to influence popular music tastes in America. Individual members of The Beatles also wrote some of the best songs of the period. And, like Elvis Presley and others before them, they set a fashion in things far beyond the music itself. Millions of teenagers, constantly seeing pop stars in the cinema, on television and on record sleeves, copied their hair styles, clothes and mannerisms. Never before had musicians made such an impact on the appearance and customs of whole generations.

Jazz, swing and the dances of Latin America like the rumba (which were also Negro in origin) influenced the very talented group of American song writers who composed music for many stage and cinema musicals between the two world wars. Irving Berlin, Jerome Kern, Hoagy Carmichael, Cole Porter, Richard Rodgers and Lorenz Hart wrote songs whose freshness and vitality were regarded as typical of the spirit of the American people, even during the years of economic depression in the 1930s, when millions of them were out of work.

George Gershwin (1898–1937) was another great American song writer of that period, but he also wanted to write music for the concert hall and opera house. In the 19th century American composers had usually gone to Europe to study and then produced music which sounded as though it had been written by a European. Edward MacDowell (1861–1908), for example, studied in France and Germany and wrote sonatas and other works which sound quite similar to the music of Liszt. Gershwin's aim was to combine European musical traditions with the rhythms and harmonies of jazz and so produce music for the concert hall as representative of his country as the music of Mussorgsky was to Russia or that of Falla was to Spain. His first and still most famous composition of this type, commissioned by Paul Whiteman, was *Rhapsody in Blue* for piano and orchestra, and the audience at the first performance in New York hailed it as a piece of music as unmistakably American as the Stars and Stripes. Gershwin's other works of the same kind include the Piano Concerto in F, the symphonic poem *An American in Paris* and his opera *Porgy and Bess*. Significantly this opera has an all-Negro cast of characters, and it contains some of Gershwin's most beautiful songs.

Gershwin did not have any academic musical training as a

young man and sometimes had to be advised on such matters as orchestration. His fellow American Aaron Copland (born 1900), on the other hand, studied music in Europe for several years. But from the start of his career he, too, recognised the importance of jazz in any attempt to create an American musical style. Copland also used American and Mexican cowboy songs and dances, and the 'hill billy' songs of the Appalachian mountains, in works like *El salón México* and the ballets *Rodeo, Billy the Kid* and *Appalachian Spring*. Roy Harris (born 1898) created in his music the same kind of vigour and feeling for the wide open spaces of the American continent.

Not only American composers were interested in jazz. In France, Debussy, Ravel and Milhaud all used jazz rhythms and harmonies in some of their music. One of Debussy's best known piano pieces is the *Golliwog's Cakewalk* from his *Children's Corner* suite, the 'Cakewalk' being an early jazz dance. Milhaud wrote music for a ballet called *La Création du monde* ('The Creation of the World'), based entirely upon jazz. The English composer Constant Lambert (1905–1951) set to music a poem by Sacheverell Sitwell called *The Rio Grande* for chorus, orchestra, piano and a large collection of jazz percussion instruments. In Germany, too, jazz had a considerable influence on the work of several composers. Ernst Křenek (born 1900) wrote an opera called *Johnny spielt auf* ('Johnny Strikes Up') about a black jazz violinist, which was very successful in the 1920s and 1930s. Kurt Weill (1900–1950) copied the instrumentation and style of jazz bands and singers in several operas he wrote in collaboration with the dramatist Bertold Brecht. The best known of these today is *Die Dreigroschenoper* ('The Threepenny Opera'), based on the 18th century English stage work *The Beggar's*

Opera. Weill and Brecht were among the large group of artists, writers and musicians who worked in Berlin in the 1920s and made the city an important centre of art and literature in the years before the Nazi rise to power.

Igor Stravinsky (1882–1971) was another European composer influenced by jazz. He wrote several pieces with titles like *Ragtime* and *Piano Rag Music*, and a jazz clarinet concerto, called *Ebony Concerto*, especially for Woody Herman. Stravinsky was born in Russia, lived in France and Switzerland for a number of years, and eventually settled in the United States, becoming an American citizen. At different times in his life he also quite drammatically changed his style of composition, just as his contemporary, the painter Pablo Picasso, progressed from one style, or period, to another throughout his life. In Stravinsky's music and Picasso's painting can be heard and seen most of the important developments in Western music and art during the first half of the 20th century.

In the years just before the First World War Stravinsky was commissioned to write three ballet scores by the Russian impresario Sergei Diaghilev. Diaghilev formed a famous ballet company and at one time or another commissioned music from Debussy, Ravel, Falla, Prokofiev, Milhaud and Poulenc; stage and costume designs from Picasso, André Derain, Henri Matisse and Georges Braque; and employed the greatest dancers of his time, including Nijinsky and Pavlova. The Diaghilev Ballet, based for most of its time in France, became a focal point for Western art and music during the early years of the century.

The first of Stravinsky's three scores for the Diaghilev Ballet was for *The Firebird*, a work based on old Russian folk tales about a fabulous bird of fire and an evil magician who turned his victims to stone. The second was *Petrushka*, the name of a traditional type of Russian puppet. In this ballet Petrushka and two puppet companions in a travelling theatre are shown living out their tragic little lives behind the stage curtain, while outside is the noise, colour and excitement of the Shrove Tide Fair in St Petersburg, the old imperial Russian capital. The third ballet was *The Rite of Spring* (also widely known by its original French title of *Le Sacre du printemps*), depicting pagan rites in ancient Russia. Stravinsky's music, from one ballet to the next, shows him progressing from

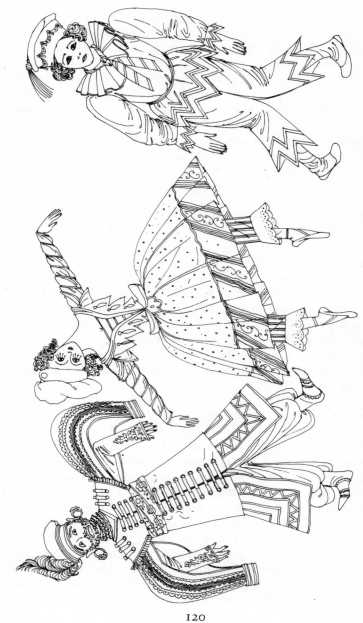

The Moor, the Ballerina and Petrushka, as they appear in Stravinsky's famous ballet

the position of a talented young composer, but one still influenced by older musicians like Rimsky-Korsakov and Scriabin, to that of a composer of outstanding originality. Indeed, the score to *The Rite of Spring* contained so many stunning new effects of orchestration, rhythm and harmony, that the first performance in Paris in 1913 ended in a riot.

Stravinsky probably realised that he had gone as far as he could in matters of orchestral complexity and dissonance with his score to *The Rite of Spring*. In the event there was no chance for him to compose anything else on similar lines, because the start of the First World War put an end to such elaborate and costly productions. So Stravinsky started writing music on a much more modest scale. For a small travelling theatre he produced *The Soldier's Tale* (called *L'Histoire du soldat* in French), based on another Russian folk tale, which has parts for only seven instruments, plus some speech and dancing but no singing. *Les Noces* ('The Wedding') is the recreation of a Russian peasant wedding, most unusually scored for a chorus, solo voices, percussion and four pianos. In these and other works Stravinsky, like other composers at that time, was turning away not just from large-scale and complex orchestral music but from the emotional intensity of Wagner, Tchaikovsky, Mahler and other late romantic composers. 'The crowd expects the artist to tear out his entrails and exhibit them,' Stravinsky said scornfully of such music. The music belonging to this creative period of his life is often described as neo-classical (or new classical) because it sounds unemotional, clear and restrained. These qualities remain even in the bigger works which Stravinsky later composed, notably *Oedipus Rex*, a kind of oratorio for the stage based on a famous tragedy from classical Greek drama, and the Symphony of Psalms for chorus and orchestra. Finally Stravinsky turned to Schoenberg's twelve-tone methods of composition, and wrote several new ballet scores based on these techniques.

Towards the end of his life Stravinsky re-visited the land of his birth. The Soviet Union had then been in existence for fifty years, and with it had been created a new kind of society. This society affected musicians, artists and writers as much as everybody else. They were supported by the institutions of the state, and in accordance with the ideas of Karl Marx, Lenin and other founder-figures of Communism, it was their duty to produce music, paintings, books or plays which would uphold the ideals of the state and also give pleasure and inspiration to the mass of the people.

Sergei Prokofiev (1891–1953) left Russia shortly after the Bolshevik Revolution of 1917 which established the Union of Soviet Socialist Republics, and composed a good deal of music which most people at the time considered very advanced and difficult. But Prokofiev had already proved what a good melodist he could be in his early *Classical* Symphony, in which he cleverly recalled something of the spirit of an 18th century symphony. So when he decided to return to his country and become a Soviet artist he again wrote music which was generally more tuneful and straightforward and intended to appeal to a wide audience. Into this category come his opera *War and Peace*, based on Tolstoy's epic novel; his music to a ballet version of *Romeo and Juliet*, and his delightful orchestral piece for children, *Peter and the Wolf*. Prokofiev also wrote music for the film *Alexander Nevsky* and for other film classics by the famous Soviet director Sergei Eisenstein.

Dmitri Shostakovich (1906–1975) was still a boy at the time of the Bolshevik Revolution, and grew up as a Soviet artist. In the 1920s artists in the Soviet Union had considerable freedom, and as a young man Shostakovich wrote some music which was as advanced and experimental as the music of Schoenberg, Bartók or, at that time, Prokofiev. But as Soviet society became more settled so its political leaders took a closer interest in what Soviet musicians, artists and writers were doing, and began to exert a greater control over their work. Shostakovich was in serious trouble when Stalin himself criticised his satirical opera *Katerina Ismailova* (originally titled *Lady Macbeth of the Mtsensk District*), and both he and Prokofiev were on several occasions accused of what the authorities called 'formalism'. By this they meant that the composers had been too concerned with the technical form of their music and so neglected its moral or social purpose.

Such criticisms did not destroy Shostakovich's belief in the Soviet way of life. He subtitled his Fifth Symphony 'A Soviet artist's reply to just criticism', and for the rest of his long and productive life worked hard to compose music which would satisfy the requirements of the state and meet his own standards and ideals as an artist. He composed fifteen symphonies altogether which are, in general, big dramatic works. Some of them were inspired by his experiences during the Second World War, and some of them have vocal and choral parts as well.

Prokofiev, Shostakovich and other Soviet composers have written much of their music in orthodox forms like the symphony, concerto, string quartet and sonata, because this was the kind of music generally approved of by the state. Many other composers of this century have also been content to create music in well established forms and according to existing conventions and rules of harmony. Hungarian-born Ernö Dohnányi (1877–1960) wrote one very popular piece called *Variations on a Nursery Theme* for piano and orchestra. The theme in question is the one known as 'Twinkle, Twinkle, Little Star', and some of Dohnányi's variations are clever imitations of other composers' styles. Paul Hindemith (1895–1963) in Germany wrote music called *Gebrauchmusik* ('utility music'), specially intended to appeal to large numbers of people or to help or instruct them in some way—ideals similar to those encouraged in the Soviet Union. Hindemith's most popular work today is his *Symphonic Metamorphoses on Themes of Carl Maria von Weber*, the rather formidable title for an entertaining piece of orchestral music.

In England, William Walton (born 1902), Michael Tippett (born 1905) and Benjamin Britten (1913–1976) have written symphonies, concertos, oratorios, songs and operas which have appealed to audiences because they could relate the music to their experience of the music of earlier composers and styles. Britten, in particular, has had great success in many parts of the world with his operas. The first of these was *Peter Grimes*, based on a rather grim poem about a Suffolk fishing village by the early 19th century English writer George Crabbe, and with it Britten did much to re-establish the reputation of English opera, after a long period of decline. He has also written much music for children to perform, and music intended for audience participation.

Other 20th century composers, however, have felt that the enormous advances in science and technology and the way these have affected people's lives should be in some way reflected by equally radical advances in music, as in painting and sculpture. The French-born composer Edgar Varèse (1885–1965) was one of these. Before the Second World War he had started writing music which went well beyond the work of other 20th century figures like Schoenberg and Bartók in breaking with past traditions. Varèse wrote one work for percussion instruments and electric sirens, and gave it the scientific sounding title *Ionisation* to suggest the startling new character of the music. He used another scientific title, *Density 21.5*, for an equally unconventional piece for solo flute. Most people did not understand or enjoy such music, and Varèse was described as very *avant-garde*—ahead of his time. The composer's uncompromising reply was that 'an artist is never ahead of his time. Most people are behind theirs!'

John Cage (born 1912), a pupil of Schoenberg, has been equally adventurous. Cage is one of several American composers who have been particularly interested in the possibility of creating new and unorthodox sounds from the piano. Earlier both Charles Ives (1874–1954), a New England businessman who was also a remarkably far-sighted musician, and Henry Cowell (1897–1966) had experimented with what are sometimes called 'tone clusters' or 'note clusters'—groups of adjacent notes on the keyboard played simultaneously with the flat of the hand or forearm. Cage himself devised what he called a 'prepared piano'—an ordinary piano with objects placed upon or between the strings in order to change their sound properties—and used this as the basis for some compositions. He conceived another piece called *Imaginary Land-scape* involving radio sets. He instructed these to be tuned to particular wavelengths and turned up or down in volume in a certain sequence. One interesting feature about such an arrangement is that on no two occasions will the radios be transmitting the same programme. Thus Cage introduced an element of chance into each performance. This chance selection of sounds is called *aleatory music*, from the Latin word *alea* meaning 'dice'. Similar, though not the same, is the principle of what is called *indeterminacy*. Here the composer leaves certain options open to the performer over such matters as where to start and end the work.

Olivier Messiaen (born 1908) of France is a composer who has created a very individual musical 'language' of his own. His fascination with bird-song has led him to re-create such sounds both for orchestral instruments and for the piano. Indian music has been another source of inspiration for him, prompting the composition of music with extremely complex rhythms. Messiaen has also written some notable organ works containing rarified harmonies and blocks of sound similar to 'tone clusters', to produce sounds very different from the kind of music most people associate with the organ. The Hungarian composer György Ligeti (born 1923) has also written organ music, sometimes so abstracted as to sound very like electronic music.

During the 1920s and 1930s a variety of musical instruments were designed to operate partly or entirely by electronic means. Examples of these are the vibraphone (very popular with some jazz musicians), Hammond organ and *ondes Martenot*. However, the age of electronic music, as most people think of it today, started soon after the Second World War, when magnetic tape recorders were invented. With a tape recorder it is possible to record any sound and then distort it in some way, for example, by playing it back at a different speed, or in reverse. And the tape itself can be cut and spliced together again, very like a strip of ciné film, thus breaking up the sounds and presenting them in a new order. Everything on the first tape can then be re-recorded on a second machine, and the process of building up new patterns of sound—rather like the way an artist builds up various colours, shapes and textures into what is called a *collage*—continues almost indefinitely.

Much early experimental work of this kind was carried out in France, where it was given the name of *musique concrète* ('concrete music'). Then a more sophisticated electronic device called a synthesizer was perfected. The name of this apparatus comes from the word 'synthesis' meaning 'build up', and it enables the operator to create instantaneously a range of sound effects which it would be quite impossible to produce on any conventional musical instrument. Synthesizers can also be used in conjunction with other electronic instruments.

Pierre Boulez (born 1925) and Karlheinz Stockhausen (born 1928)—both pupils of Messiaen—Luciano Berio (born 1925), Hans Werner Henze (born 1926) and Krystof Penderecki (born 1933) are leading composers of today who have all made extensive use of electronic techniques. Stockhausen was the first composer to devise a method of presenting an electronic 'score' in the form of diagrams, since ordinary notation would be quite inadequate for the purpose. He has also been at pains to stimulate interest in electronic music. His work called *Kontakte* is for electronic sounds, piano and percussion instruments. His object here, as he has explained, is that the familiar sounds of the piano and percussion should 'function as traffic signs in the unlimited space of the newly discovered electronic sound world'. Another very interesting work by Stockhausen is *Stimmung* ('mood' or 'atmosphere'), in which one basic chord produced by six vocalists is constantly changed and modified electronically like some slowly shifting kaleidoscopic light pattern.

A piece like *Stimmung* does not stimulate the mind or the senses in the way that most music does. On the contrary, it can bring about a state of almost complete mental passivity, or stillness, at which point normal thought processes are suspended. This is moving into the region of *psychedelic art*. The word 'psychedelic' comes from two Greek words—*psyche*, 'soul' or 'mind', and *deloun*, 'to reveal'—and means mind-expanding or mind-revealing. Progressive pop groups, who also produce electronic music, are concerned with this. They often give themselves strange or outlandish names, like *Soft Machine, Pink Floyd, Egg, Led Zeppelin, Tangerine Dream*, which are themselves intended to help shake the mind out of its normal association of ideas.

Sometimes their music sounds hard and relentless and is often played at an extremely high volume so that it has the effect of stunning a person's senses and in this way breaking down the ordinary condition of thinking and feeling. But progressive pop music can be soft, strange and ethereal, like *Stimmung*, washing the listener's mind clear and so opening the way to new states of awareness.

Pop group in full electronic swing

For a long time people have spoken of music as an 'international language', because Britishers and Frenchmen, Russians and Germans, Italians and Poles could all perform and enjoy each other's music, even if they could not understand one word of each other's spoken language. Until recently this idea of the international appeal of music hardly took into account the music of North Africa and the Middle East, of India and China, where most of the people on this planet actually live. Today, though, the people of Europe, and of those countries like the United States which have a largely European cultural background, are less parochial in their outlook. Through jazz, the music of Africa and of black men and women has come to play an important part in their lives. And today, in cities like London, Paris and New York, recitals of Indian music attract large audiences; while musicians from China, Japan and Korea are now celebrated performers of Western music.

Much of today's most interesting new music takes all these

developments into account. At the same time, the old distinctions between 'serious' and 'popular' music (which were always rather misleading) are now becoming increasingly blurred under the impact of musical techniques and ideas from all corners of the earth. So music really does seem to be emerging as an international kind of language. The problem for both musician and music-lover today is in trying to keep pace with a musical language which also seems to be growing and changing at a speed appropriate to the Space Age!

Some Well-known Musical Terms and Expressions, with a simple pronunciation guide

Many of these terms indicate speed or mood and are often combined as a general instruction at the start of a piece of music, e.g. *allegro con brio, andante cantabile*. All are Italian, since this language has long been accepted as the standard one among musicians, although expressions and terms in German, French, English and other languages do, of course, exist.

a tempo (ah *tem*-poh)   at the original speed
accelerando (a–chel–lay–*ran*–doh)   accelerate, speed up
adagio (a–*dar*–jee–oh)   fairly slow
adagietto (a–dar–jee–*et*–oh)   little adagio, not quite so slow
allegro (a–*leg*–roh)   fairly fast
allegretto (a–lay–*gret*–oh)   little allegro, not quite so fast
andante (an–*dan*–tay)   leisurely, moderate speed
andantino (an–dan–*tee*–noh)   little andante, slightly faster
animato (an–ee–*mah*–toh)   animated, lively
arco (*ah*–coh)   instruction to string players to resume playing with the bow after playing pizzicato
arpeggio (ah–*pej*–ee–oh)   notes of a chord spread out, played one after the other, as they often are on the harp
cantabile (can–*tah*–bee–lay)   in a singing style
coda (*coh*–dah)   a tail-piece, a concluding passage
con amore (con ah–*mor*–ay)   lovingly, tenderly
con brio (con *bree*–oh)   vigorously
con fuoco (con foo–*ock*–oh)   with fire, passion
con moto (con *moh*–toh)   with movement, a good sense of pace
con spirito (con *spee*–ree–toh)   with spirit
crescendo (cresc.) (cray–*shen*–doh)   getting louder
da capo (d.c.) (dah *cah*–poh)   repeat from the beginning
diminuendo (dim.) (dee–min–oo–*en*–doh)   getting softer

dolce (*dol*-chay)   soft, sweet, gentle

dolente (doh-*len*-tay)   sad, wistful

forte (f) (*for*-tay)   loud

fortissimo (ff) (for-*tiss*-ee-moh)   very loud

giocoso (jo-*cos*-soh)   merry, playful

glissando (glee-*san*-doh)   quickly up or down the notes of a scale

largo (*lah*-goh)   very slow

larghetto (lah-*geh*-toh)   little largo, not quite so slow

legato (leh-*gah*-toh)   smooth, flowing, succession of notes played without a break between them

leggiero (lej-ee-*air*-roh)   light, delicate

lento (*len*-toh)   slow

maestoso (my-*stos*-soh)   majestic, grand

mezzo forte (mf) (*met*-soh *for*-tay)   half loud, i.e. not too loud

mezzo piano (mp) (*met*-soh pee-*ah*-noh)   half soft, i.e. not too soft

nobilmente (no-bil-*men*-tay)   nobly, grandly

non troppo (non *trop*-poh)   not too much, with regard to speed

obbligato (ob-lee-*gah*-toh)   special or significant part written for an instrument in any piece for more than one instrument or voice

ostinato (os-tee-*nah*-toh)   a constantly repeated phrase, often as the accompaniment to a melody

pesante (peh-*san*-tay)   heavily, gravely

piacevole (pee-ah-*chay*-voh-lay)   pleasing, pleasant

piano (p) (pee-*ah*-noh)   soft

pianissimo (pp) (pee-ah-*niss*-ee-moh)   very soft

pizzicato (pizz.) (pit-see-*cah*-toh)   playing a bowed stringed instrument by plucking the strings

poco a poco (*poh*-coh ah *poh*-coh)   little by little, gradually

portamento (por-tah-*men*-toh)   carrying, i.e. sliding up from one note to another, especially as practised by string players and singers

presto (*press*-toh)   fast

prestissimo (press-*tiss*-ee-moh)   very fast

rallentando (ral-len-*tan*-doh)   slow down

ritardando (ritard.) (ree-tah-*dan*-doh)   slow down

ritenuto (ree-ten-*oo*-toh)   hold back the speed

ritornello (ree-tor-*nel*-loh)   a recurring passage, often between the verses of a song

rubato (roo-*bah*-toh)   a manner of playing, holding on to some notes and skipping over others, stretching and condensing the speed

scherzando (skairt-*san*-doh)   light-hearted, lively

sforzando (sf) (sfort-*san*-doh)   forceful, with special emphasis, applying to a note or chord staccato (sta-*cah*-toh)   detached, note or notes sounded crisply and separately from each other. Indicated by a dot over the note or notes in question

sostenuto (sos-ten-*oo*-toh)   sustained, played smoothly

stretto (*streh*-toh)   at a faster speed

tremolo (*trem*-oh-loh)   rapid repetition of the same note, especially in the case of bowed stringed instruments, to create a trembling effect

tutti (*too*-tee)   all together

vibrato (vee-*brah*-toh)   rapid fluctuations of pitch around one note, especially as practised by singers and players of bowed stringed instruments

vivace (vee-*vah*-chay)   lively, bright

INDEX